the yarn girls' guide to simple knits

the yarn girls' guide to simple knits

Julie Carles and Jordana Jacobs

photographs by Dorothy Handelman
illustrations by Daniela Tineo & Gael Cadden
additional photographs by Cappy Hotchkiss

Clarkson Potter / Publishers
New York

Text copyright © 2002
by Julie Carles and Jordana Jacobs

Photographs copyright © 2002 by Dorothy Handelman

Published by Clarkson Potter/Publishers, New York, New York.

Member of the Crown Publishing Group, a division of Random House, Inc.

www.randomhouse.com

CLARKSON N. POTTER is a trademark and POTTER
and colophon are registered trademarks of Random House, Inc.

Printed in China

Design by Lauren Monchik

Library of Congress Cataloging-in-Publication Data
Carles, Julie.
The yarn girls' guide to simple knits / Julie Carles and Jordana Jacobs.—1st ed.
p.   cm.
1. Knitting—Patterns.   2. Sweaters.   I. Jacobs, Jordana.   II. Title.
TT825 .I87   2002
746.43'20432—dc21

2001050031

ISBN 0-609-60880-0
10 9 8 7 6 5

acknowledgments

We would like to thank so many people for making this book possible: Petra Marcel for things so numerous that we cannot even begin to try listing them here. Deb Futter for encouraging us to take the chance and just write a proposal. Dorothy Handelman for the beautiful photography and Tisha Brown for being a great stylist. Daniela Tineo for her wonderful illustrations. Carla Glasser for shopping our proposal around and trying to smooth over the rough edges. Irina Poludnenko for helping us knit all the sample sweaters. Also we would like to thank our families, Mort, Nancy, and Matt Israel and Jack, Marcia and Daniele Merlis—and the new additions to our families, our husbands—John Carles and Jeff Jacobs. Finally, we would like to thank all of our great customers who have encouraged us, tried out these patterns, and waited patiently for the publication of this book. Thank you.

Contents

introduction 8

the yarn girls' guide to the fundamentals 11

slip knot and cast on 12

knit and purl 16

ribbing 20

increase and decrease 22

bind off 26

yarn overs 28

fringe 29

single crochet and shrimp stitch 31

finishing techniques 34

gauge page 41

knitting glossary 44

the yarn girls' favorite patterns 47

funnel-neck pullovers 54

even daniele did it 56

a tempting turtleneck 59

funky funnel-neck fun 62

crewneck pullovers 66

don't be a football widow 68

the weekend warrior 72

trick or treat 75

cardigans 79

the problem solver 80

give the people what they want 83

a craving to knit 87

v-neck pullovers   93
stripes are stars   94
not your standard-issue sweatshirt   97
bare that belly   100
tank tops   105
oooh baby   106
sexy summer tank   109
summer in the city   112
men's sweaters   117
he'll wear it every day   118
the compromise   121
the exception to the rule   124
hats   129
jeff's striped hat   130
the knitting club's hat   132
feeling fuzzy   134
scarves   137
hole-in-one   138
airy wrap   139
the chunkiest of the chunky   140
ponchos   143
easy, breezy, beautiful   144
winter poncho   146
rectangles only   148
throws   151
bulky blanket   152
design your own throw   154
how deena got her ooohs and aaahs   156
resources   158
index   159

introduction

If you've picked up a fashion magazine or wandered into
a department store lately, chances are you've noticed that great sweaters are
everywhere. Bulky and roomy or silky and clingy, they're as right for the
office as they are for the summer cottage. If you're anything like us, you want
them all. The good news is that unlike the intricately patterned intarsia knits
or tricky bobbled and cabled numbers your grandmother seemed to produce
with ease (and which then languished at the back of your closet), these fabulous sweaters are surprisingly easy to make. Their enormous appeal comes
from their rich colors, flattering shapes, and sexy textures, not complicated
stitches or shaping.

As owners of The Yarn Company, a busy yarn shop located on the Upper
West Side of Manhattan, we realized our customers were looking to knit
sweaters that blended seamlessly into their existing wardrobes without scream-
ing "homemade"—and that could be started and completed in less time than
it takes to grow out a bad haircut. Yet even we found it was virtually impossi-
ble to locate stylish, simple, quick-to-knit sweater patterns. So, being resource-
ful types (with wardrobe needs of our own), we took the matter into our own
hands and designed a group of sweater patterns using yarns that we loved
working with. We even took things one step further and designed some acces-
sories to go with our sweaters as well as some beautiful throws for the home.
The response has been great and, best of all, the ease of completing these
projects has encouraged a lot of knitting novices to expand their limits and
even brought many lapsed knitters back into the fold!

In *The Yarn Girls' Guide to Simple Knits* you'll find easy-to-knit patterns
for the six most popular sweater shapes. We have included patterns for the
newly popular funnel-neck pullovers as well as the traditional standbys:
crewneck pullovers, V-neck pullovers, cardigans, tank tops, and the comeback
kid . . . ponchos. We also offer patterns for scarves, hats, and throws. And, we
have even included a few sweaters for a man in your life.

We believe that options are key. So, we offer three different takes on each
basic design, showing how these shapes can look radically changed when you
play with the yarn, gauge, or other details like neckline or ribbing. For example, one crewneck pullover has a wide rib with a mock turtleneck, another
has a foldover turtleneck, and the third is a standard pullover without ribbing
around the bottom or sleeves. These slight variations in the pattern, along

with the use of different yarns, create three sweaters that have very individual looks, yet are based on essentially the same template.

All the sweaters knit up quickly—we know, we knit them—and we have made the instructions as user-friendly as possible. Because you may be new to knitting (or need a quick refresher course), we have defined absolutely every knitting term that might cause confusion. In other words, if the pattern tells you to SSK, you can find out what the heck SSK means and you can also learn how to SSK. (Incidentally, you will find this technique illustrated on page 25.) And each sweater pattern has its own "cheat sheet"; you won't have to worry about shaping an armhole on only one side of your sweater if you follow these step-by-step guides.

We have written this book as a basic primer of knitting techniques and we hope you use it as such. Please heed the wisdom contained in the helpful hints we've scattered throughout the book; most of these address mistakes that we have seen and even made a hundred, if not a thousand, times. Some may seem obvious, but in the end, they will save you from knitting a sweater that would fit the Jolly Green Giant or, worse, one with armhole shaping only in the back! We have designed our patterns to address potential pitfalls in advance so you never have to suffer the indignity of ripping out many, many hours of hard work.

So, let your imagination go. Be creative and mix and match our patterns. We will be so, so proud of you, and you'll have a sweater like no one else's. Even if you've never knit anything more ambitious than a potholder in Girl Scouts—or anything at all—we can help you create a sweater that looks like it came out of the pages of *Vogue* in a matter of days, and better yet, at a fraction of the price. Best of all, you'll get the incomparable thrill of having someone ask you, "Where did you get that fantastic sweater?" and be able to answer smugly, "Oh, it's just something I made myself."

Happy knitting.

—Julie and Jordana

the yarn girls' guide to the fundamentals

Has it been a long time since you picked up a pair of knitting needles? If so, you may be a bit rusty on the rudiments. Face it, we all get confused and forget things we have learned—even if we just learned them yesterday. Our goal is to make knitting as easy as possible, and to enable you to create a sweater—start to finish—without a million trips to your local knitting store or tears and frustration. This chapter provides instructions on the basic techniques that we use throughout the book. If you are a new knitter, or if you're a bit out of practice, this is where you'll turn for directions on how to knit, purl, cast on, and bind off. If you have forgotten how to make a slip knot or do a rib stitch, if you're not sure how to increase, or decrease, bind off, or any of the other fundamental tools for making a knitted garment, you're in the right place. And whether this is a refresher course or your first foray into the pleasures of knitting, we promise to keep it simple.

By the way, for you lefties out there, don't be intimidated. These directions are universal and we teach righties and lefties to knit exactly the same way. If, however, you feel you want to alter the motions slightly to compensate, go ahead—just do what feels comfortable for you.

You may also have seen or heard about the "European method" of knitting, in which you knit with yarn wrapped around your left index finger, to make a new stitch rather than wrapping the yarn around the needle with the right hand. All the illustrations and instructions in this book are based on the American method, which is how we knit and what we teach our students. If you already know how to knit in the European method, continue to do so if that's what you're comfortable with—these patterns will work equally well for you. Just make extra sure your gauge is correct.

Even before you begin to knit, you must cast the necessary number of stitches onto your needle. To do this, you have to measure out a length of yarn for a "tail" which will become your cast-on stitches. The length of the tail determines how many stitches you can cast on; the more stitches you are casting on, the longer the tail must be. Our rule of thumb is that an arm's length, that is, the distance from your wrist to your shoulder, of yarn will yield 20 stitches on the needle. So, if you need to cast on 100 stitches, you'll need to use 5 arm lengths of yarn. It is always better to have too long a tail than one that is too short. If your tail runs out before you have cast on the required number of stitches, you will have to start over with a longer tail. You can always cut the remaining yarn off if the tail is too long, but always leave at least two or three inches.

After you measure out the tail, make a slip knot in one end, which will also be your first cast-on stitch. Place this on a needle, hold that needle in your right hand, and continue to cast on stitches until you have the required number on the needle.

this is where it all begins

to make a slip knot

Measure out the required length of yarn and, with the free end hanging, make a loop at the measured point. You should see an "X." (Illus. A)

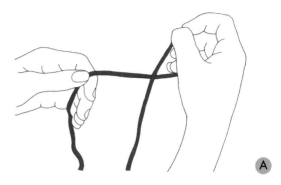

A

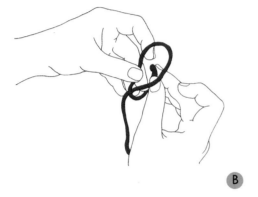

B

Grab hold of the strand of yarn that is on the top of the "X" and bring this strand behind and through the loop. (Illus. B)

Hold this new loop in one hand and pull on the loose ends to create your slip knot! (Illus. C & D)

C

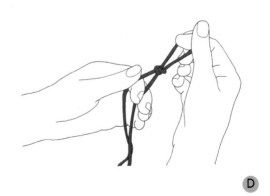

D

to cast on

Place your slip knot on a needle. Hold the needle in your right hand pointing toward the left. Hold the slip knot in place with your right index finger so it does not fly off the needle. (Illus. A)

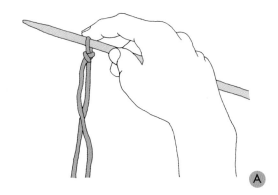

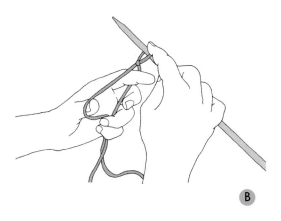

Place the thumb and index finger of your left hand in between the 2 strands of yarn dangling from the needle. (Your thumb should be closer to you and the index finger away from you.) Hold the dangling yarn taut with your ring and pinky fingers. (Illus. B)

Flip your left thumb up while guiding the needle down and to the left. A loop should form around your thumb. (Illus. C)

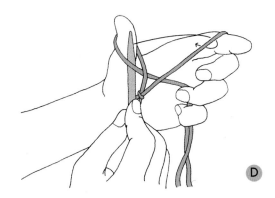

Guide the needle up through the loop on your thumb. (Illus. D)

Guide the needle over the yarn that is around your index finger and catch it with the needle. (Illus. E)

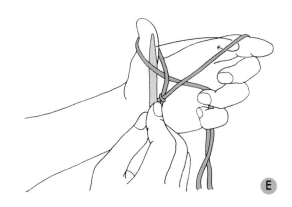

E

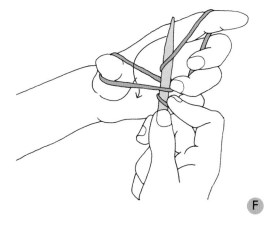

F

Guide the yarn hooked by the needle down through the loop around your thumb. (Illus. F and G) Slip your thumb out of its loop and place this thumb inside the strand of yarn that is closer to you. Pull down gently and you have a cast-on stitch!

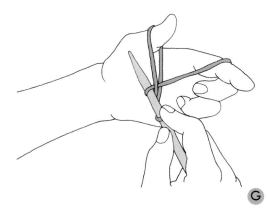

G

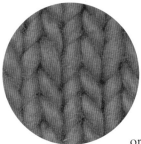

Knit and Purl

Knit and purl are the two stitches that make up the craft of knitting—everything else is merely a variation on one or both of these two stitches. Once you master the knit and purl stitches, the world of knitting is yours to conquer.

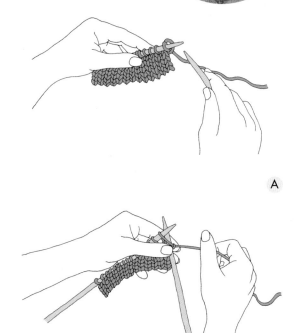

to knit

Cast on the number of stitches required by your chosen pattern or 20 stitches if you are just practicing. Hold the needle with the cast-on stitches in your left hand and the empty needle in your right hand. Point needles toward each other. (Illus. A)

A

While holding the yarn in the back, insert the right needle from front to back through the first stitch on the left needle. You will see that the needles form an "X" with the right needle beneath the left needle. (Illus. B)

B

C

Keep the needles crossed by holding both needles with the thumb, index and middle fingers of your left hand. Do this by holding the right needle with the thumbnail on top facing you, and the nails of the index and middle fingers underneath that right needle and facing away from you. With your right hand, pick up yarn and wrap the yarn counterclockwise under and around the bottom needle; do not wrap it around the left needle. (Illus. C)

Hold the yarn in place around the right needle in between your right thumb and index finger and guide the right needle toward you through the center of the stitch on the left needle. (Illus. D) The right needle should now be on top of the left needle. (Illus. E)

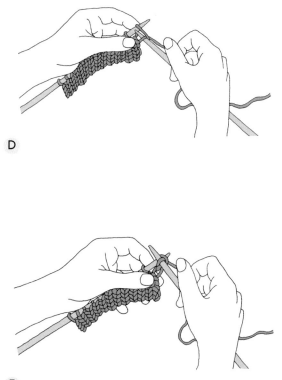

D

Pull the remaining yarn off the left needle by pulling the right needle up and to the right so that the newly formed stitch slides off the left needle to the right. You will have a newly created stitch on the right needle. (Illus. F)

Repeat steps 1 through 5 across the entire row of stitches.

E

NOTE: When you finish knitting the entire row, all of your stitches will now be on the right needle. Switch hands, placing the empty needle in your right hand and the needle with the stitches on it in your left hand. Now you are ready to begin knitting another row.

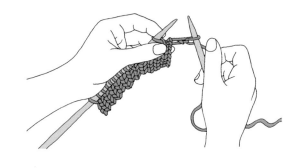

F

to purl

Hold the needle with the stitches in your left hand and the empty needle in your right hand and the loose yarn hanging in front of your work. The needles should be pointed toward each other. (Illus. A)

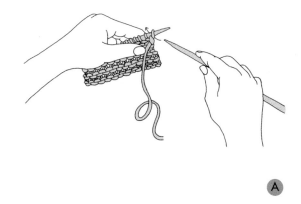

A

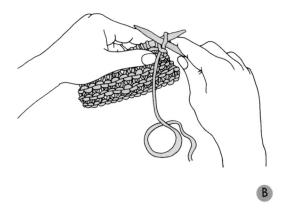

B

Insert the right needle back to front through the front of the first stitch on the left needle. The needles will form an "X" with the right needle on top of the left needle. Make sure that the yarn is in front of the needle. (Illus. B)

Keep the needles crossed in the "X" position by holding both needles with the thumb, index, and middle fingers of your left hand. Do this by holding the right needle with the thumbnail on top facing you, and the nails of the index and middle fingers underneath that right needle and facing away. Wrap the yarn counterclockwise around the front needle from the back, bringing the yarn around and in front of the right needle. (Illus. C)

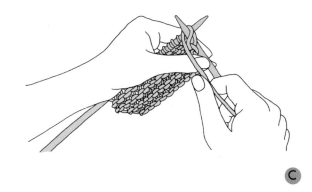

C

Holding the yarn in place around the needle with the thumb and index finger of your right hand, push the right needle down and toward the back through the center of the stitch on the left needle. The right needle will now be behind the left needle. (Illus. D & E)

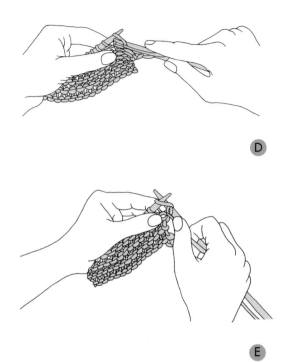

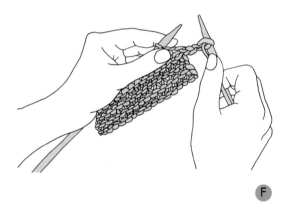

Pull the remaining yarn off the left needle by pulling the right needle to the right so that the newly formed stitch slides off the left needle onto the right needle. (Illus. F)

Now you know how to knit and purl. If you alternate knitting a row and purling a row you will be working in the most commonly used stitch, the stockinette stitch. This is universally abbreviated as St st. If you just knit or just purl on every row then you are working in a garter stitch.

Stockinette can be achieved by the knit stitch alone when you knit in the round. Knitting in the round is exactly what it sounds like. Instead of knitting a row and transferring the stitches from one needle to another, you knit continuously in a circle. The most common uses for this are making hats, socks, and adding roll neck edges to sweaters.

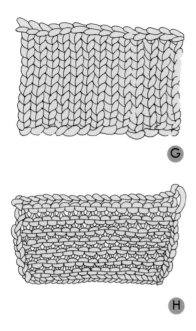

(G)

(H)

To achieve a garter stitch when knitting in the round, you need to alternate knitting one round and purling one round.

So, what would happen if you stopped working on your practice swatch and came back to it a few days later? Would you know what to do next? Look at both sides of the piece you have done so far. One side has stitches that resemble V's. (Illus. G) The other side should look like horizontal bars or maybe tiny pearls. (Illus. H) The V's are the knit stitches, the horizontal bars are the purls. So pick up your swatch. Place the empty needle in the right hand and the full needle in the left hand. Look at what is facing you. If the V's are facing you, then you are ready to do a knit row. If the horizontal bars are facing you, you are ready to do a purl row.

If you get interrupted in the middle of a row, it gets a bit trickier. Just remember that the needle with the ball of yarn attached should be in your right hand and the other needle in your left hand. Then look at the stitches and follow the rule above.

Ribbing

When you knit and purl stitches next to each other in the same row, and then follow the pattern on the next row by knitting over your knit stitches and purling over your purls, you will create a ribbing. You can do a Knit 1, Purl 1 ribbing or a Knit 2, Purl 2 ribbing or any such variation. The key to making a ribbing is remembering that the yarn must be in *back* of your right needle when you are knitting and in *front* of your right needle when you are purling. In this book we often begin sweaters with a ribbing. It makes a nice border and prevents the edges from curling. You can also make a whole sweater with a rib pattern. The illustrations here show a Knit 2, Purl 2 ribbing.

Knit 2 stitches. (Illus. A)

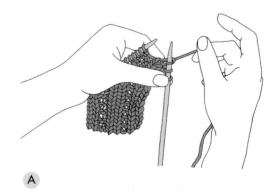

(A)

B

Separate the needles slightly and bring the yarn from the back of your work to the front. Be sure that you bring the yarn in between the needles and not over a needle (which would cause you to add a stitch). (Illus. B)

Purl 2 stitches. (Illus. C)

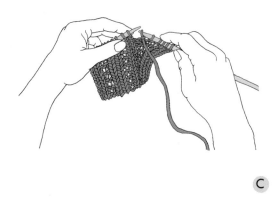

C

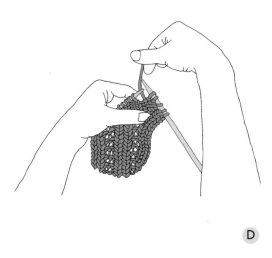

D

After purling, you must bring the yarn in between the needles to the back of the work before you knit 2 stitches again. (Illus. D)

Repeat these steps for your ribbing. Note how knit stitches (V's) are over knit stitches and purl stitches are over purls. (Illus. E)

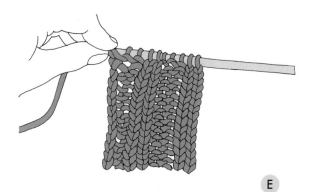

E

Increase and Decrease

Unless you are knitting a scarf, a blanket, or something else that is the same width from start to finish, you will need to add and subtract stitches during the course of your knitting project. The addition and subtraction of stitches is otherwise known as increasing and decreasing. While it is possible to increase and decrease on either the knit or the purl side of your work, there is rarely a need to do so while purling. The illustrations here show how to increase and decrease on the knit side.

INCREASING

Increasing is how you will add stitches to the number of stitches on a needle in order to add width to your knitted piece. The most common reason for increasing is shaping sleeves. A sleeve must start out narrow and get wider as it gets longer. This is accomplished by adding 1 stitch to each end of the needle every several rows.

You will encounter two methods for increasing in this book. The first is the bar method, known as Make 1, or **M1,** which is our preferred way to increase while knitting sleeves. Generally we recommend that you start a bar increase 2 stitches in from the edge of your work. This means that you should knit 2 stitches, then do a bar increase, then knit until there are 2 stitches remaining on the left needle, then increase again. Increasing 2 stitches in from your edge makes sewing up the seam on your sleeve much easier, because it allows you to sew down a straight line that is uninterrupted by increases.

The second kind of increase is known as knitting into the front and back of a stitch. It is a quick and easy way to increase and is generally a good choice when you want your increases at the very edge of the knitted piece. We don't like this increase for sleeves because it tends to leave a slightly jagged edge that makes sewing more difficult; however, we used this method for the ponchos on pages 145 and 147 because these edges don't get sewn up.

bar method
(also referred to as make 1, or m1)

At the point where you wish to add a stitch, pull the needles slightly apart to reveal the bar that is located in between 2 stitches. (see arrow, Illus. A)

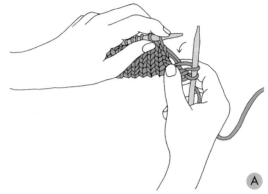

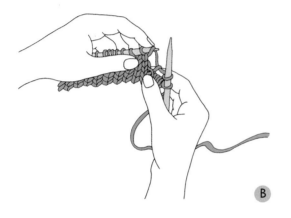

With your left needle, pick up the bar from behind. (Illus. B)

Knit the loop you have made. Be sure to knit this loop as you would normally knit a stitch, going from the front of the stitch to the back. (Illus. C) Sometimes this stitch is a little tight and will be difficult to knit. In that case, gently push the loop up with your left forefinger, loosening the stitch and making it easier to insert your right needle.

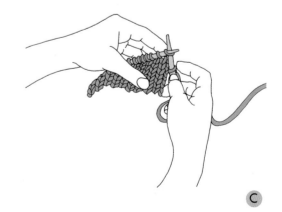

knitting into the front and back of a stitch

Begin to knit into the stitch that you are going to increase into. Stop at the point when you have brought the right needle through the stitch on the left needle and it is forming the "X" in the front. (Illus. A) DO NOT take the stitch off the left needle as you normally would when completing a knit stitch.

Instead, leave the stitch on the left needle and move the tip of the right needle so that it is behind the left needle. (Illus. B)

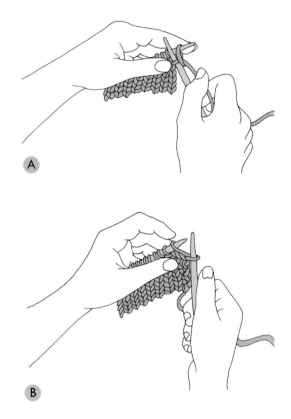

Insert the right needle into the back of the stitch on the left needle (Illus. C) and knit it again—wrap yarn around the back needle counterclockwise. Hold the yarn against the needle with your right hand and guide the needle toward you through the center of the stitch. The right needle should end up on top of the left needle.

Pull the stitch off the left needle. You now have 2 stitches on the right needle. (Illus. D)

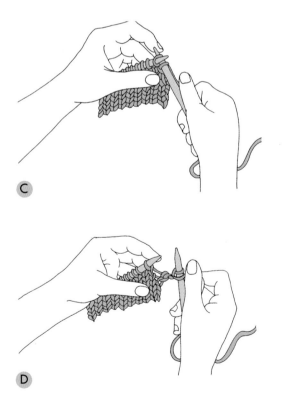

DECREASING

Decreasing is how you will *reduce* the number of stitches on a needle in order to narrow the width of your knitted piece. The most common use for decreases is shaping armholes and necks.

In this book we use two methods of decreasing. The first is a slip, slip, knit, abbreviated as **SSK.** This is a left-slanting decrease. The other method is a Knit 2 together, abbreviated as **K2tog.** This is a right-slanting decrease.

slip, slip, knit (ssk)

We use this method when we want our decreases to slant toward the *left*.

One at a time, slip 2 stitches, as though you were going to knit them (Knitwise), to the right needle. (Slipping a stitch means that you insert your right needle into the loop on the left needle as though you were going to knit it BUT you don't complete the knit stitch, you just slide the stitch off the left needle onto the right needle.) (Illus. A)

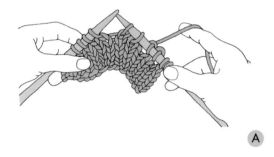

A

Insert the left needle into the front of the 2 slipped stitches, forming an "X," with the left needle in front of the right needle. (Illus. B)

Wrap the yarn counterclockwise around the back needle and knit the 2 slipped stitches together (Illus. C), slipping the completed new stitch onto the right needle.

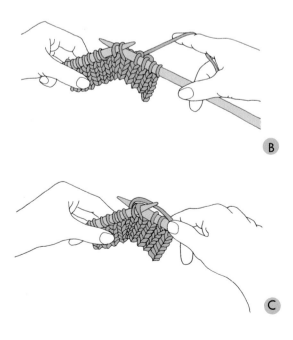

B

C

knit 2 together (k2tog)

We use this technique when we want our decreases to slant to the *right*.

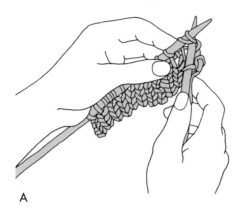

A

Working on a knit row, insert your right needle from front to back into the second and then the first stitch that you want to knit together. (Illus. A)

Bring the yarn around the needle and complete the stitch as though you were knitting a regular stitch. (Illus. B)

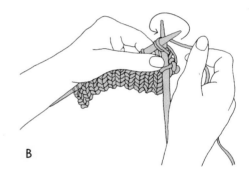

B

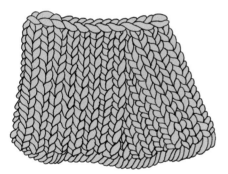

Bind Off

Binding off is how you get your knitted piece off the needles and prevent it from unraveling. You bind off when you are finished with your scarf, when you are shaping a neck or armholes, or when you have completed the front or back of a sweater. We will explain what shaping a neck and shaping an armhole mean later on; for now, all you need to learn is how to bind off. You can bind off on a knit or a purl row. The concept is the same either way. We illustrate how to bind off on a knit row.

Knit 2 stitches. (Illus. A)

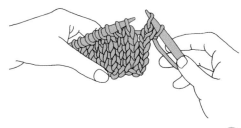

A

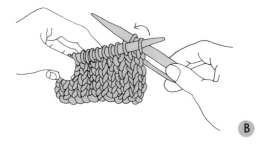

B

Insert the left needle into the front of the first stitch on the right needle. Using the left needle, pull the first stitch up and over the second stitch. (Illus. B) You can place your forefinger on the second stitch to hold it in place to keep it from coming off the needle.

Now push that stitch off the left needle completely. (Illus. C & D)

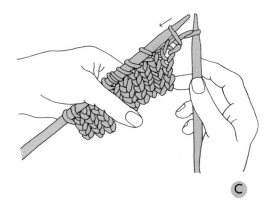

C

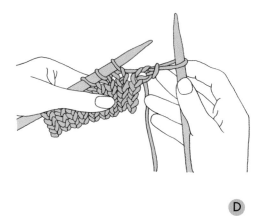

D

Knit one more stitch and repeat the last two steps. Continue this process until you have bound off the desired number of stitches.

When you are binding off all your stitches at the end of a scarf or blanket or when you are done knitting a section of your sweater, you should have 1 loop left on the right needle. At this point, cut the yarn, leaving 3 or 4 inches, and pull the end through the remaining loop in order to tie it off.

Yarn Overs

A yarn over (abbreviated **YO**) basically allows you to make a hole in your knitting on purpose—as opposed to those inadvertent holes that are made by dropping stitches. Yarn overs are generally used for lace knitting or to make a buttonhole.

yarn over before a knit

If the stitch after the yarn over will be a knit, you will use this method of making a yarn over:

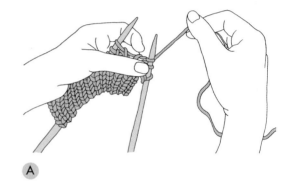

Hold both needles with the fingers of your left hand and hold the yarn with your right hand in back of the right needle. (Illus. A)

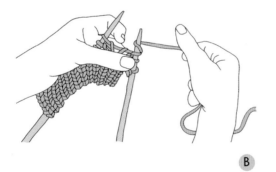

Pull the yarn up and around the right hand needle from the front to the back. (Illus. B) You created the yarn over, which is just a loop.

yarn over before a purl

If the stitch after the yarn over will be a purl, use this method:

Hold both needles with the fingers of your left hand and hold the yarn with your right hand in front of the right needle. (Illus. A)

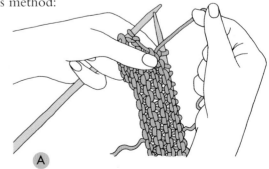

Pull the yarn up and around the needle counterclockwise, from the front to the back and to the front again. (Illus. B)

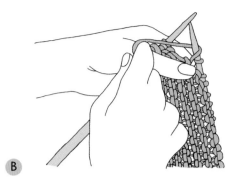

B

ℭringe

Fringe is a nice accent to scarves, ponchos, and throws.

Before you start making fringe you will need a few things: a piece of cardboard, a crochet hook, a pair of scissors, and your yarn.

Once you have your materials, determine how long you want your fringe to be. Next, cut a piece of cardboard as tall as the fringe's length. (You can also use a found object that fits your size requirements; we sometimes use our checkbook or a calculator.) If you are going to be a stickler regarding the length of your fringe, it may be a good idea to cut the cardboard a bit longer than you actually want the fringe—you can always trim it if it's too long. The first step in making fringe is wrapping the yarn around the cardboard approximately 20 times. (If you need more, you can repeat this step.) Then cut the strands of yarn across the top of the cardboard. You now have strands of yarn that are twice your desired length. If you want thick fringe, take several strands of yarn, if you want thinner fringe, take only a strand or two.

To attach fringe to your knitted garment, insert your crochet hook through a stitch at one of the ends of your knitted piece. You should take the crochet hook from underneath the piece to the top of it and the crochet hook should be facing you. (Illus. A)

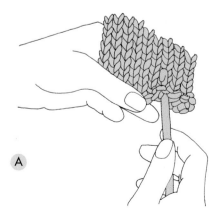

A

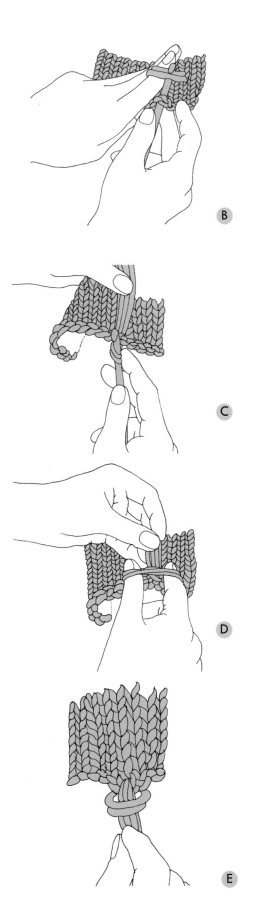

VERY IMPORTANT:
To fill in the fringe on a piece of work, we suggest you start by attaching fringe at each edge and then at each midway point until you are satisfied.

B

C

Fold your strands of yarn in half and grab the center of these strands with your hook. Pull these strands through the stitch. (Illus. B & C)

Remove the crochet hook and place your fingers through the loop you made with the strands of yarn. Then pull the loose ends through this loop. (Illus. D & E)

You have completed one fringe. (Illus. F) Cut the ends to even off if you prefer.

D

E

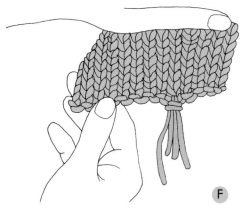

F

Single Crochet and Shrimp Stitch

Even if you have never crocheted—and never plan to—it's useful to know a couple of basic crochet techniques for finishing off a knitted piece. Using a crochet stitch for edgings gives sweaters and throws a nice, polished look. Shrimp stitch gives a sturdy corded look. You must do a row of single crochet (abbreviated **SC**) before you can add your shrimp stitch. Generally, you want to use a crochet hook that matches the size knitting needle you used. For instance, if you used a size 6 knitting needle, you should use a size 6 (also known as size G) crochet hook.

single crochet

With the right side of the work facing you, insert your crochet hook through a stitch under the bind off. (Illus. A)

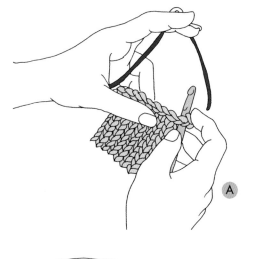

Grab the yarn with the crochet hook and pull it through the stitch to the front of your work. (Illus. B) You will now have 1 loop on the crochet hook. (Illus. C)

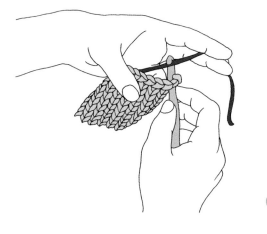

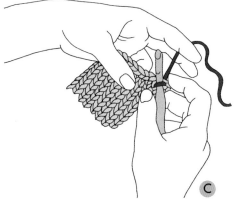

31

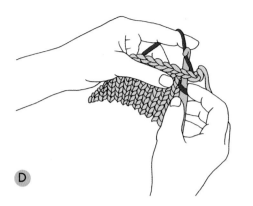

D

E

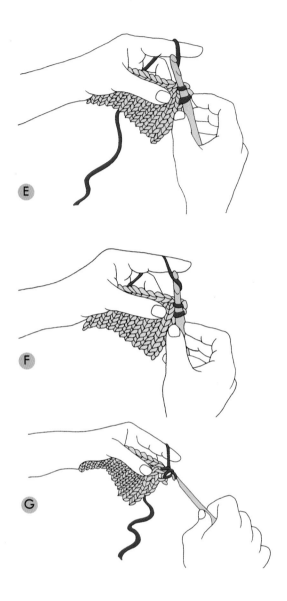

F

G

Insert the crochet hook through the next stitch, hook the yarn, and pull it through the stitch. You will now have 2 loops over the crochet hook. (Illus. D & E)

Hook the yarn and pull it through both of the loops on the crochet hook. (Illus. F & G) You will end up with 1 loop on the hook. Insert the hook through the next stitch and repeat across the entire row, ending with 1 loop on the hook.

shrimp stitch

This is also known as backwards crochet because you work from left to right instead of right to left. You must do 1 row of single crochet before you begin the shrimp stitch.

Make a slip stitch by grabbing the yarn through the loop on the hook. (Illus. A)

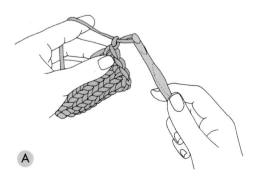

A

Keeping your right index finger on the loop, insert the hook into the next stitch to the right from the right side to the wrong side of the work. (Illus. B & C)

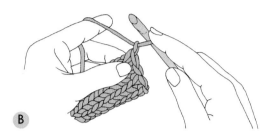

B

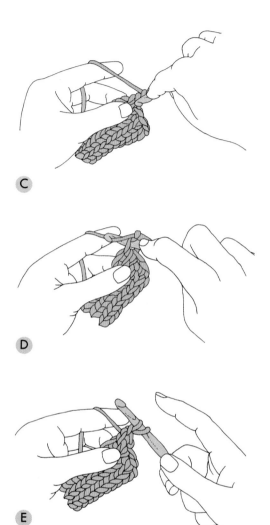

C

D

Grab the yarn with the hook and pull it through to the right side of the work. (Illus. D)

You should have 2 loops on the hook. (Illus. E)

E

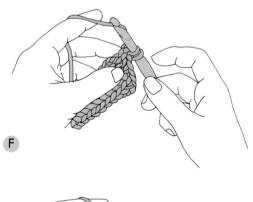

F

Grab the yarn with the hook and pull it through the 2 loops. (Illus. F & G)

Repeat in the next stitch to the right. (Illus. H)

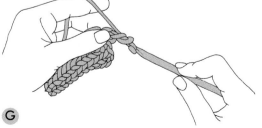

G

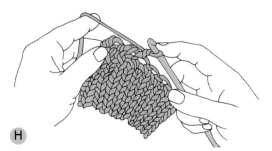

H

Finishing Techniques

You can spend hours knitting row after row of perfect ribbing and flawless stockinette stitch, but all those efforts can be undermined by sloppy finishing technique. Knowing how to sew a sweater together properly is the ultimate key to whether the sweater looks handmade— or homemade. Finishing a sweater is the bane of many a knitter's existence, but it doesn't have to be. If you use the proper techniques, the process should be relatively painless and your sweater should look virtually seamless. And a final steaming, known as blocking, will smooth over any inconsistencies or bumpy seams.

Some tips:

- This may go against every instinct that you possess, but sweaters are always sewn on the right side. This means that unlike regular sewing, where the two right sides of your garment are facing each other when you sew, in knitting **the right sides face out.**

- Although other people might tell you differently, we prefer **not** to use the yarn we knit our sweater with to sew it together. If your garment is sewn together properly, you will not see any of the yarn used for sewing on the right side. This means, theoretically, that you should be able to sew your black sweater together with hot pink yarn. Generally, we suggest using a needlepoint yarn in a similar color because using a different yarn allows you to see what you are doing much better. And, dare we say it, it also enables you to rip out what you have done if necessary without inadvertently damaging the sweater itself.

Whether making a V-neck, turtleneck, crewneck, or cardigan, sweaters are always assembled in the same order:

1. Sew shoulder seams together.
2. Sew sleeves onto sweater.
3. Sew sleeve seams from armhole to cuff.
4. Sew side seams from armhole to waist.

Once the pieces are joined together, you can add crochet edgings, pick up stitches for a neck, create button bands for a cardigan, or other finishing touches.

sewing shoulder seams

Lay the front and back of your sweater flat with the right sides facing you and the shoulders pointing toward each other. If you are sewing the shoulder seams of a cardigan together, make sure that the neck and armholes are facing in the correct direction, with the armholes facing away from the center and the neck toward the center. (Illus. A)

Cut a piece of sewing yarn approximately twice the width of your shoulder seam and thread it through a darning needle.

Secure the sewing yarn to the garment by making a knot with one end of the sewing yarn on the inside shoulder edge of the back of your sweater.

Insert the needle into the first stitch at the shoulder edge of the front of the sweater. Your needle should have passed under 2 bars and should be on the right side or outside of the work. (Illus. B)

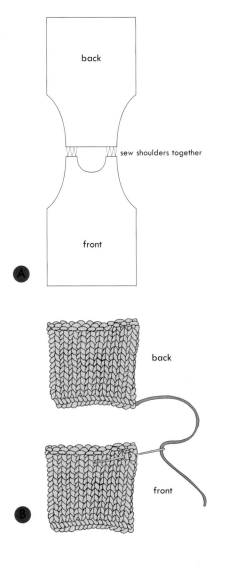

Now place the needle under the corresponding stitch of the back of your sweater. (Illus. C) Next your needle will go into the hole that the yarn is coming from on the front and you will go under the next stitch. You will do the same thing on the back now. This is how you continue to weave the sweater together. It is easier if you keep the yarn relatively loose because it is easier to see the hole that your yarn is coming from. Pull the sewing yarn tight after you have 6 or 7 stitches and just loosen the last stitch before you proceed.

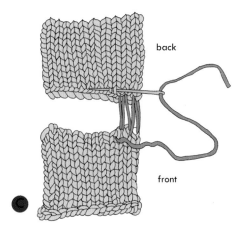

sewing the sleeves to the body

This is possibly the most difficult aspect of finishing your sweater because it is really the only part where something must fit into something else. The cap of your sleeve must fit *perfectly* into your armhole. That said, sometimes it is possible to fudge it a little to make it work.

Cut a piece of yarn approximately 30" long and thread it through a darning needle.

Attach the yarn to the body of the sweater by poking the needle through the edge of the shoulder seam that you made when sewing the shoulders together. Pull the yarn halfway through and make a knot. You should now have half the yarn going down one side of the armhole and half going down the other side.

VERY IMPORTANT: You must keep checking to see if the sleeve is going to fit into the armhole. If it won't fit perfectly into the armhole, you can make adjustments. Ease the sleeve in by taking 2 bars from the longer edge and only 1 bar from the shorter edge. Do this a few times and check again. Repeat this until the two fit together. If it really seems hopeless, take out what you have sewn and start again, making adjustments from the beginning.

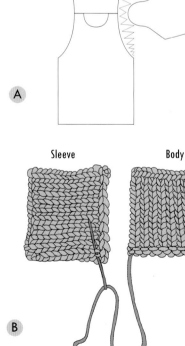

A

Find the center of the upper sleeve edge by folding the sleeve in half. With the yarn needle, pull the yarn under the center 2 bars on the sleeve. (Illus. A) Your sleeve is now attached to the body of the sweater.

Now you need to find 2 bars on the body of the sweater. Start at the top near the shoulder seam. This is slightly different from finding the bars on the sleeves because the bars on the sleeves are stitches and on the body, the bars will be rows. Place the needle 1 full stitch in on the body of the sweater and find the 2 bars. (Illus. B)

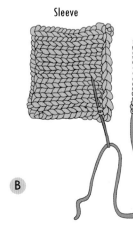

Sleeve   Body

B

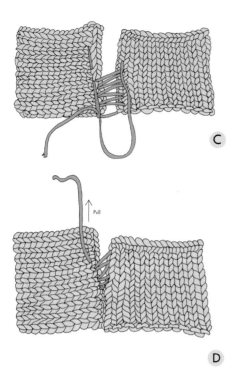

Continue sewing as for the shoulders, taking 2 bars from the body and 2 bars from the sleeve and pulling the yarn every few stitches until the sewing yarn is no longer visible and until the sleeve is sewn into the armhole. (Illus. C & D)

sewing side & sleeve seams

Cut a piece of yarn approximately twice the length of the sleeve and side seam.

Attach the yarn by inserting the needle through the two seams at the underarm. Pull the yarn halfway through and make a knot. Half of the yarn should be used to sew the side seam and half should be used to sew the sleeve seam.

It doesn't matter whether you start with the body or the sleeve. For both, find the 2 vertical bars 1 full stitch in from the edge and begin the sewing process, (Illus. A) taking 2 bars from one side of the sweater then 2 bars from the other side. (Illus. B) Make sure you are going into the hole where the yarn last came out and pulling the yarn every few stitches. (Illus. C)

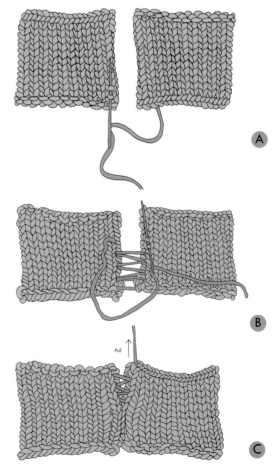

picking up stitches

Once the pieces of your sweater are joined together, you need to make a nice finished edge for the neckline. If you are making a cardigan, you will also need to add button bands on each side, one with buttonholes and the other a solid strip to which you will attach the buttons. Rather than knit these elements as separate pieces that are then sewn on, we like to knit them directly onto the finished sweater. In order to do this, you must pick up stitches along the finished edges. When you pick up the stitches for a neck, you are generally picking up stitches horizontally, in an already-made stitch. When picking up for button bands, you pick up the stitches vertically, in rows. Either way, the method for picking up the stitches is the same; the difference is where you place the needle to pick up the next stitch. You can pick up stitches in existing stitches (horizontally Illus. A–E) or in rows (vertically Illus. E–J).

Place work with the right side facing you. Starting at the right edge of your piece with the knitting needle in your right hand, place the needle into the first stitch, poking through from the outside to the inside. (Illus. A & B; F & G)

Loop the yarn counterclockwise around the needle and pull the needle back through that same stitch. There should be 1 stitch on the needle. (Illus. C & D; H & I)

Continue to poke the needle through each stitch, wrapping the yarn around the needle as if you were knitting, and adding a stitch to the needle each time. (Illus. E & J)

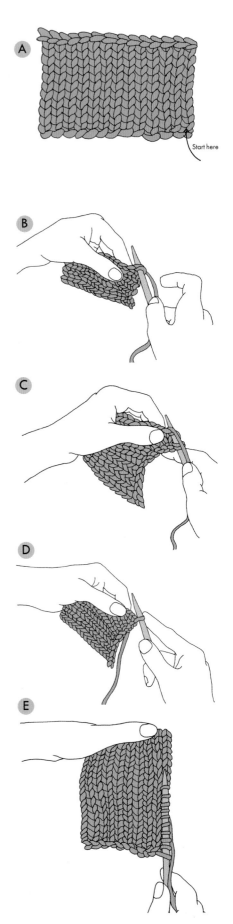

A

Start here

B

C

D

E

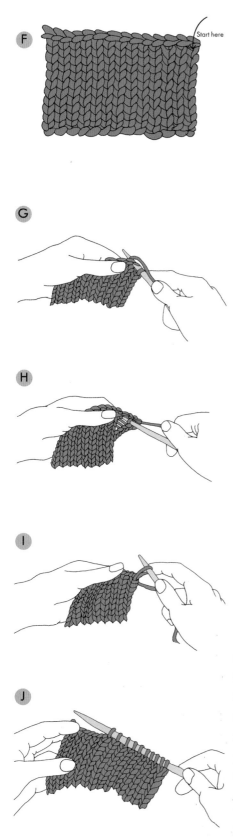

F

Start here

G

H

I

J

When you are picking up stitches in stitches, as for a crewneck pullover, most of the time you want to pick up every stitch. It is very important to note that there is an extra hole in between each stitch. So picking up every stitch is the same thing as picking up every other hole. If you poke your needle through every consecutive hole, you will have picked up too many stitches.

When you are picking up stitches in rows, as when you are picking up button bands, you do not want to pick up a stitch in every row. To determine how often to pick up, note your gauge. If your gauge is 3 stitches to the inch, then you will want to pick up stitches in 3 consecutive rows and then skip 1 row and continue to repeat this process. If your gauge is 4 stitches to the inch, you will want to pick up stitches in 4 consecutive rows and then skip 1 row. It is necessary to skip a row every so often because there are more rows per inch than stitches per inch. If you were to pick up a stitch in every row, when you started to knit these picked-up stitches, you would have too many stitches and the button bands would look wavy.

blocking

Sometimes when a garment is completely assembled, it requires a bit of shaping. Blocking allows you to gently reshape the piece by applying steam, which relaxes the yarn fibers so they can be stretched in order to smooth out bulky seams, even out uneven knitting, or even enlarge a too-small garment.

Not every piece needs to be blocked; use your common sense. But if you do decide some reshaping or smoothing is in order, pin your garment onto a padded ironing board, easing it into the desired shape. If your iron can emit a strong stream of steam, hold the iron above the piece without touching it and saturate it with steam. Otherwise, dampen a towel, place it over the garment, and press with a warm iron. Allow the piece to remain pinned to the ironing board until it is completely cool.

Never apply a hot iron directly to a knitted piece, and always read the label on your yarn before blocking; some fibers should not be blocked.

gauge page

THE MOST IMPORTANT MESSAGE IN THIS
CHAPTER IS THAT YOU MUST ALWAYS MAKE A
GAUGE SWATCH! IF YOU DON'T MAKE A
GAUGE SWATCH, THERE ARE NO GUARANTEES
THAT YOUR SWEATER WILL FIT PROPERLY!

You just spent time and money picking out yarn to make a sweater. You're eager to get to work and most of all, you can't wait to try your handiwork on and have it fit perfectly—as if it were made for you! In order for this scenario to have a happy ending, it is crucial that you understand gauge. A grasp of gauge will save you from the misery of having to rip out your knitting because your hoped-for size small looks like it could fit the circus fat lady. And it will help you avoid the depression that comes from investing hours of time on an unwearable garment. If you're not yet a master of gauge, read this information carefully!

STITCH GAUGE = THE NUMBER OF STITCHES
REQUIRED TO PRODUCE 1 INCH OF KNITTED
FABRIC

Gauge is the most important—and most misunderstood—element of knitting. Simply put, stitch gauge determines the finished measurements of your garment. Technically, and yes, it is a technical, even mathematical concept, stitch gauge tells you the number of stitches you'll need to knit to produce a piece of knitted fabric that is 1 inch wide.

For each pattern in this book you will find a diagram, also called a schematic, that indicates the garment's finished measurements. If your gauge is off, the finished knitted piece will not have the proper dimensions for the size you have chosen. It is, therefore, important to refer back to these finished measurements as you knit, making certain your gauge has not changed and that the finished piece will have the correct measurements.

A pattern is always written with a specific gauge in mind, and if you do not get the gauge just right, your project won't turn out as the pattern designer intended.

Here's a simple example: If a pattern says your stitch gauge should be 3 stitches to the inch, that means 60 stitches should produce a piece of knitted fabric that is 20 inches wide. This is because 60 stitches divided by 3 (your gauge) equals 20 inches. If your gauge were 4 stitches to the inch, you would need to cast on 80 stitches to produce the same 20-inch width.

It really is just that easy, simple division and multiplication, and you can even use a calculator—we do!

All patterns state the stitch gauge (or tension, if it's not an American pattern) required to achieve the desired measurements for your finished garment. The gauge swatch is always knit in the same stitch you'll use for the garment itself. Usually a pattern will tell you that your stitch gauge should be measured over 4 inches (or 10 centimeters if, again, it's not American). For example, under gauge your pattern may say 16 stitches = 4 inches. This means that your stitch gauge should be 4 stitches to the inch. Patterns also generally include a row gauge, which indicates how many rows you need to knit in order to get a piece of knitted fabric 1 inch long. For most of the patterns in this book, row gauge is not particularly important, so you really only have to worry about stitch gauge.

Along with the gauge, patterns also tell you what needle they recommend to get a particular stitch gauge with a particular yarn. DO NOT assume that just because you are using a pattern's suggested yarn and needle size that you

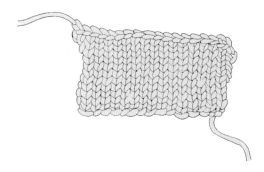

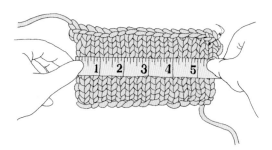

don't have to do a gauge swatch. Everybody knits differently. Some people are loose knitters, some are tight knitters, and some are in the middle. Whatever type of knitter you are, you can always get the required gauge eventually, but you may need to make some adjustments. Tight knitters will have to go up in needle size, while loose knitters will have to use needles a size smaller. Remember, it's far more important to get the specified gauge than to use the specified needle, or yarn for that matter.

Here's how to check your gauge:

- Cast on 4 times the number of stitches required per inch. For example, if the gauge is 4 stitches = 1 inch, cast on 16 stitches; if your gauge is supposed to be 3 stitches = 1 inch, cast on 12 stitches.
- Work in the pattern stitch using the needle size required for the body of the sweater. Sometimes ribbing is knit on smaller needles, but don't use the smaller size for your gauge.
- When your gauge measures approximately 4 inches long, slip the swatch off the needle and gently place it on a flat surface. Measure the width of your swatch. If your swatch measures 4 inches wide, you're getting the required gauge and can begin your knitting project.
- If your swatch is more than 4 inches wide your knitting is too loose. Reknit your gauge on needles a size or two smaller, and measure the swatch again. Repeat as necessary, using smaller needles until you get the gauge.
- If your swatch is less than 4 inches wide, you are knitting too tight. Reknit your gauge on needles a size or two larger, and measure the swatch again. Repeat as necessary, using larger needles until you get the gauge.

REMEMBER—ALWAYS KNIT A GAUGE SWATCH—ALWAYS!!

You should also know that gauge can change as you make your garment. This happens for a multitude of reasons and does not mean you are a bad knitter. Please check the width of what you are knitting once the piece measures about 3 inches long. Compare it to the measurements that the pattern provides and make adjustments in the needle size if necessary.

BIND OFF (CAST OFF) This is the way you get stitches off the needle at the end of a project. Cast off is also a method used to decrease stitches.

CAST ON This is how you put stitches onto your needle to begin a project.

DEC. Decrease. This is how you take stitches away once you have begun knitting. We use two methods of decreasing in this book, SSK & K2tog.

EDGE STITCH An edge stitch is exactly what it sounds like, the stitch that is at the edge of your work. Some of our patterns call for an edge stitch and this means that we want you to knit the first and last stitch on every row, no matter what the rest of the pattern requires.

GARTER STITCH Knit every row. But if you are knitting in the round (on a circular needle), then garter stitch means you should knit 1 round and purl the next.

INC. Increase. This is how you add a stitch onto your needle once you have begun knitting. We use two methods of increasing in this book, a bar increase (Make 1, abbreviated M1) and knitting into the front and back of a stitch.

K Knit.

K2TOG Knit 2 stitches together. This is a method of decreasing. It slants your decrease toward the right.

P Purl.

REV ST ST Reverse Stockinette Stitch. P 1 row, K 1 row, and the purl side is the "right side" of the garment.

RS Right Side. This is the side that will face out when you are wearing the garment. In this book, the RS is always the knit side.

SC Single crochet.

SEED STITCH Seed stitch is like a messed-up ribbing. Like ribbing you alternate knitting and

purling, but instead of knitting on the knit stitches and purling on the purl stitches to create ribs, you purl over your knit stitches and knit over your purl stitches to create little "seeds."

SSK Slip, Slip, Knit. This is a method of decreasing. It slants your decrease toward the left.

ST ST Stockinette stitch. Knit 1 row, purl 1 row. But if you are knitting in the round (on a circular needle), then St st means you should knit every round.

WS Wrong Side. This is the side that will face in when you are wearing the garment. In this book, the WS is always the purl side.

YARN DOUBLED When you knit with the yarn doubled, you are working with 2 strands of yarn held together as though they were 1. **Yarn tripled** means working with 3 strands of yarn held together. It is no harder to knit with 2 or 3 strands of yarn than it is to knit with 1. When we tell you to use a yarn doubled or tripled, it means that the yarn we used for the pattern needed to be thicker than it actually is in order to achieve the proper gauge. If you prefer not to double or triple yarn, try substituting a bulkier yarn that knits to the gauge with a single strand. Just remember that if you use a single strand of yarn where we used 2, you will need only half the yardage to complete the pattern, or one third if the yarn is tripled.

YO Yarn Over. This is how you make a hole in your work (on purpose). Yarn over is often used in lace knitting, but in this book we use it to make a small hole in our angora scarf, and we recommend that you use yarn overs for your buttonholes.

...... In knitting patterns, asterisks are used to indicate that a series of stitches is to be repeated. Repeat only what is between the asterisks, not what is outside of them. For example, **K2, *K2, P2* 3** times means K2, K2, P2, K2, P2, K2, P2. ***K5, K2tog* across row** means that you should K5, K2 tog, K5, K2 tog, and so on across the whole row.

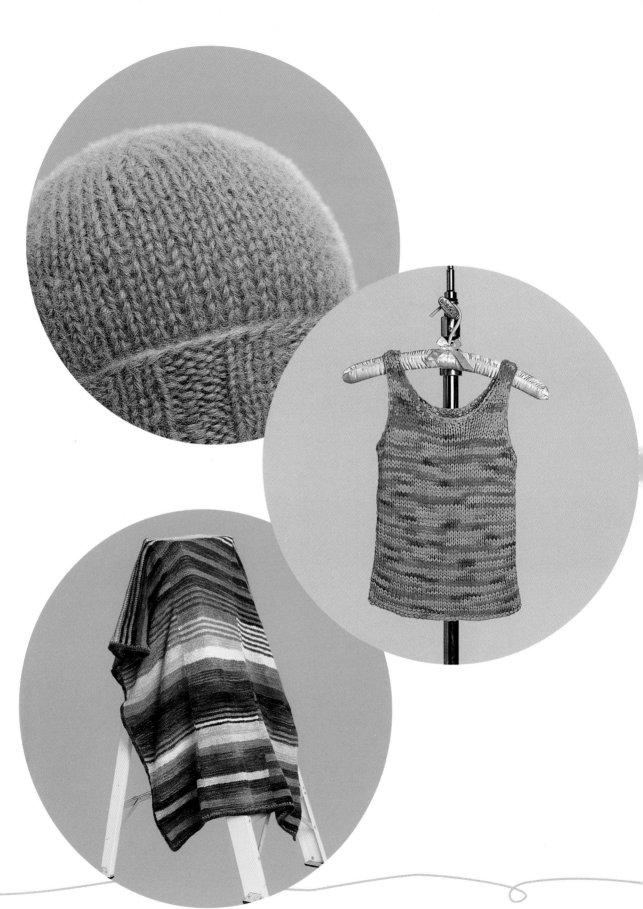

the yarn girls' favorite patterns

Finally, the good part—the patterns. You'll notice there are three patterns for each of the ten basic shapes. Each pattern in a given group is distinct from the next because it's knit in a different gauge and because we've interchanged the details such as cuffs, collars, and finishing touches. These simple variations make each garment look unique, despite the fact that they're based on a common template. That means that if you can make the "Problem Solver" cardigan you can make "Give the People What They Want" too! Each time you master one version of a design, you've really mastered all three! Yet no one will know you're essentially making the same garment over and over again; they'll only notice the lovely textures and finished details.

For each of the patterns that follow we provide the general instructions that tell you what type of yarn to use and how much of it you need. We then provide directions for knitting the sweater in three sizes, small, medium, and large. Directly after each pattern are step-by-step guides that focus on the trickier aspects of making the projects. The step-by-steps are there to help you with such things as shaping the armhole, crewneck, or V-neck. If you follow these instructions to the letter, you should be able to master the procedure even if you are a novice who has never done any kind of shaping before. At the same time you will be creating a lovely and wearable piece of knitted clothing!

The beauty of these patterns is their versatility. Once you're comfortable with a given pattern and have mastered its more challenging elements, you can get a little creative. Try mixing and matching different edgings or necks, or make the crewneck sweater you love as a turtleneck. You can also try out new stitches and apply them to a basic project shape. Just remember, you still must get the correct gauge in your pattern stitch.

We want your knitting to go as smoothly as possible so please read the tips that follow *before* you knit. It beats having to come back later searching for a clue to what went wrong after you've put in several hours on your project.

SOME WORDS OF WISDOM

Make sure you have *all* the materials required before you start your project. Knitting patterns are like recipes in that everything you need to make the finished product is listed at the beginning. Your pattern should tell you the required stitch gauge, the recommended needle size, the type of yarn used, the number of balls needed, the yardage per ball, and the finished measurements of the garment.

Make sure you knit a gauge swatch to guarantee that you are getting the required stitch gauge. (Obviously, we can't stress this enough.) Also, in order to get a good fit you should always know the finished measurements of your garment. Knitting patterns always state these, either on a diagram or written out. You should measure the width of the piece you are knitting every few inches to ensure that you will in fact produce a piece of knitted fabric that conforms to the specified measurements of the project you are making. Even if you got the gauge when you knit your gauge swatch, check the measurements along the way. Sometimes people knit their actual garments tighter or looser than they did their swatch. This happens to the best of us, so always remeasure and make adjustments if necessary. If your measurement is *not* correct, you *must* rip out the knitting you have done (if you've been measuring all along, it will be only a few inches) and start over. Go down a needle size or two if the garment is too big and up a needle size or two if it is too small.

Before you start knitting, read over your pattern. Make sure that the actual knitting instructions make sense to you. See if you understand the abbreviations and techniques that are used. If you are confused by anything, you have several options:

- Remember that your knitting book is your best resource. In this book and most other knitting books there is a glossary that defines and explains the various techniques and abbreviations used (see page 44). If you don't remember what WS stands for, you can turn to the glossary and it will tell you that WS means wrong side. It will also explain what wrong side means. If you are confused by something more complex, such as how to do an SSK, refer to the diagram in the how-to section.

- You can cross-reference. If you find the definitions in a given book to be unclear, check out another book. Knitting books often explain things slightly differently and one book might provide an explanation that is easier for you to understand than another. Also, remember that people learn things in different ways. Some are very visual and looking at a diagram is all they need in order to figure something out. Others do better by reading written instructions, and some need someone to actually show them how things are done. If you are one of the latter, don't hesitate to march back down to the store from which you purchased your yarn to get a few pointers.

- Sometimes things just don't make sense until you actually do them. You can always knit your project up to the point where things start to get bewildering, then read the pattern carefully and work *exactly* as instructed—even if you can't quite visualize the outcome. You'll be surprised how often things make sense after you've done a row or two.

- Don't freak out when you finish a ball of yarn. It is easy to add a new ball. Just tie the ends of the old and new balls together with a double knot, leaving strands that are long enough to weave in on both. Try to attach the new ball at the end of a row, not in the middle. If you can't you can't—but if you aren't sure the yarn you have left will make it across the row, be safe and start a new ball.

Common sense is perhaps the most important thing to rely on when knitting a pattern. Don't blindly follow a pattern that your gut tells you is wrong. That is a recipe for disaster. Always look at what you are doing and ask yourself if it looks correct. Does it look too big or too small? Is it lopsided? Don't you need armholes on *both* sides of your sweater? Simple common sense may help you avoid pitfalls. Don't be afraid to trust your instincts.

> Don't blindly follow a pattern that your gut tells you is wrong. That is a recipe for disaster.

CHOOSING YARN FOR YOUR SWEATER

For many knitters, the second most exciting part of a project (after getting big compliments the first time you wear it!) is picking out the yarn. There are so many delicious new yarns on the market today, in lush colors and irresistible textures, you may feel like a kid in a candy store when you shop for your yarn. We do, and we own the candy store!

We have noted the specific yarn we used for each pattern, as well as the number of balls we used and the yardage. However, if you can't find the same yarn for any reason—it could be discontinued, or your shop just might not carry it—you can easily substitute yarns, as long as you choose a yarn or combination of yarns that gets the same gauge as the yarn we used. The key below will help you substitute yarns.

Also, just because we used double strands of yarn doesn't necessarily mean that you must. If you prefer to substitute a yarn that knits to the required gauge using a single strand, that's okay. Just be sure that when you choose a different yarn, you base the amount you will need on the yardage and not on the number of grams or balls. For example, if we use 10 balls of yarn that have 100 yards in each ball and we are knitting with a *single strand* of yarn, we are using 1,000 yards of yarn. If the yarn you like has 75 yards per ball, you will need 14 balls. Or, if we use 15 balls of a yarn that has 100 yards and we are using a *double strand* of yarn, we are using 1,500 yards. But if you want to use a yarn that gets the same gauge with a single strand and it has 75 yards per ball, you will need only 10 balls.

A FEW LAST THINGS BEFORE YOU BEGIN

The following are some terms you may encounter in the knitting patterns in this book. Read through this section before you start a project so that when you encounter a reference to reverse shaping or see an asterisk in your knitting directions it won't throw you for a loop.

knitting markers

When you need to mark off a designated number of stitches on your needle, say to mark the center of a V-neck, you may be instructed to place a marker on the needle. You can buy markers at your yarn shop, or just make your own by tying a short strand of yarn in a color that contrasts with your piece into a loop.

needle size

Needles come in all different sizes from less than 0 all the way up to 50. Your needle size helps determine your gauge (see the Gauge Page), and you need to use different size needles with different yarn weights and thicknesses. A size 0 needle has a very small diameter and is used with very, very fine yarns to make very tightly textured, fine work, especially for baby clothes. A #7 needle is a medium-size needle that is generally used with medium-weight yarn. A #50 needle looks like a turkey baster and is used with incredibly chunky yarn or many strands knitted together at once. This produces a very thick knitted fabric.

reverse shaping

We use this term when we want you to make two pieces, one the mirror image of the other. When you shape the neck on a pullover, you bind off the center stitches and then finish one side of the sweater at a time. On one side you will have to shape the neckline in one direction (while knitting) and on the other side it will have to be shaped in the other direction (while purling). Also, when you make a cardigan, you make two front sections—one that will be the right side when worn and one that will be the left side when worn—and must shape the necklines and armholes in opposite directions. The easiest way to visualize this is to shape one side without really thinking about it and then, when you get to the neck shaping on the second side, lay both pieces out as they would be on the finished sweater. You will see what the second neckline needs to look like.

yardage

Yardage helps you determine how many balls of yarn you will need for your project. Many books and patterns tell you that you need a certain number of grams or ounces, but in our experience this is an inaccurate way to determine the amount of yarn you will need, as different fibers have different weights. Acrylic is a much lighter fiber than wool: A 50-gram ball of acrylic yarn might contain 200 yards, whereas a 50-gram ball of wool might only contain 125 yards. Therefore, if a pattern called for 200 grams of acrylic yarn and you bought 200 grams of wool instead, you would be 300 yards short and would be very upset when you could not complete your last sleeve. In this book, we always specify the total number of yards needed for each pattern.

Good luck, and we hope you enjoy knitting these patterns.

KEY TO YARN WEIGHTS

Although every project in this book is knitted with yarn that is considered chunky, not all chunkies are created equal—some are so bulky that a single stitch equals one inch when knitted.

At the beginning of the instructions for each project you will see a ball of yarn. This indicates the approximate weight of the yarn used and the gauge as listed below; note that when the piece was knitted with doubled or tripled yarn, we indicate this also.

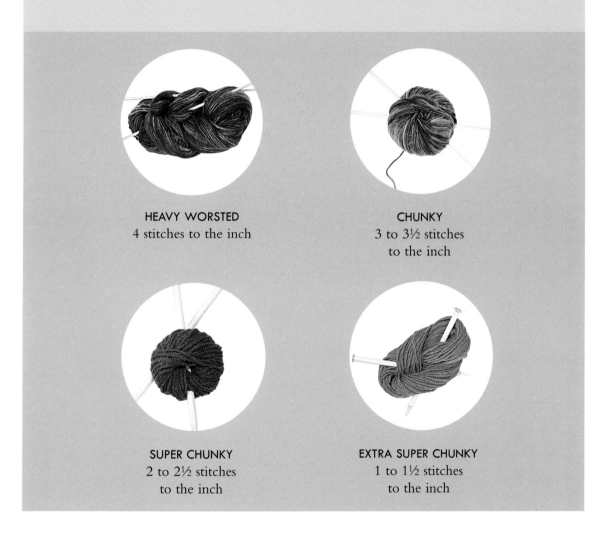

HEAVY WORSTED
4 stitches to the inch

CHUNKY
3 to 3½ stitches
to the inch

SUPER CHUNKY
2 to 2½ stitches
to the inch

EXTRA SUPER CHUNKY
1 to 1½ stitches
to the inch

Funnel-Neck Pullovers

Funnel-neck sweaters are great beginner projects.

They are fast and very fashionable. Their main advantage is that they require no neck shaping and there is no need to pick up stitches. The idea behind the funnel neck is that you bind off the stitches for the shoulders at the beginning of two consecutive rows and then you continue knitting on the remaining stitches to create the neck.

    Even Daniele Did It is a turtleneck with stockinette stitch at the neck. *Funky Funnel-Neck Fun* is a roll neck, and *A Tempting Turtleneck* is a ribbed turtleneck with ribbing at the bottom and sleeves as well. Try one, try them all. They're *that* easy.

even daniele did it

Daniele was a spaz knitter. Every time she made something, it came out wrong. One sleeve was longer than the other, the neck was too low, or the sweater was too long, too short, too loose, or too tight. Finally, we urged Daniele to try this sweater, because so many people make it and it looks great on everyone. We were willing to bet she would find success at last.

We were right! Not for nothing is this our most popular sweater! Daniele knit up a killer sweater in a matter of days and it looks fabulous on her. Beginner knitters like it because it is knit on really big needles and has no ribbing or neck shaping. And it's equally popular with experienced knitters who want to curl up on their couch for the weekend and go to work on Monday wearing their newest creation.

YARN: Muschio (39 yards/50g ball)
COLOR: Dark Gray #354
AMOUNT: 12 (13, 14) balls
TOTAL YARDAGE: 468 yards (507 yards, 546 yards)
GAUGE: 2 stitches = 1 inch; 8 stitches = 4 inches
NEEDLE SIZE: US 15 (10mm) or size needed to obtain gauge
SIZES: S (M, L)

back and front (make 2):

With #15 needle, cast on 40 (44, 48) stitches. Purl 2 rows. Then continue in St st until piece measures 14″ (15½″, 17″) from cast-on edge, ending with a WS row. **SHAPE ARMHOLES:** Bind off 3 stitches at the beginning of the next 2 rows. Bind off 2 stitches at the beginning of the next 2 rows. Then decrease 1 stitch at each edge every other row 1 (2, 3) times until 28 (30, 32) stitches remain. Continue to work in St st until piece measures 23½″ (25″, 27″) from cast-on edge. **FUNNEL NECK:** Bind off 6 (7, 7) stitches at the beginning of the next 2 rows. Continue to work in St st on remaining 16 (16, 18) stitches for 6 more rows. Purl 1 row on knit side of work. Continue to work in reverse St st for 10 rows. Bind off loosely.

sleeves (make 2):

With #15 needle, cast on 20 (20, 22) stitches. Purl 2 rows. Then continue in St st. At the same time, increase 1 stitch at each edge every 10th (10th, 6th) row 5 (5, 6) times, until you have 30 (30, 34) stitches. Continue in St st until sleeve measures 15″ (16″, 18″). **NOTE:** Increase leaving 2 edge stitches on either side of work. This means you should knit 2 stitches, increase a stitch, knit to the last 2 stitches, increase a stitch, and then knit the remaining 2 stitches. Increasing like this makes it easier to sew up your seams. **SHAPE CAP:** Bind off 3 stitches at the beginning of the next 2 rows. Bind off 2 stitches at the beginning of the next 2 rows. Then decrease 1 stitch at each end every other row 1 (2, 3) times. Bind off 2 stitches at the beginning of the next 4 (6, 6) rows. Bind off remaining stitches.

finishing:

Sew shoulder seams together. Sew sleeves on. Sew side and sleeve seams.

1: KNIT ROW: Bind off 3 stitches, knit to end.
2: PURL ROW: Bind off 3 stitches, purl to end.
3: KNIT ROW: Bind off 2 stitches, knit to end.
4: PURL ROW: Bind off 2 stitches, purl to end.
5: KNIT ROW: Knit 1 stitch, K2tog, knit until 3 stitches remain on left needle, K2tog, K1.
6: PURL ROW: Purl.
Repeat rows 5 & 6 0 (1, 2) more times.

1: KNIT ROW: Bind off 6 (7, 7) stitches, knit to end.
2: PURL ROW: Bind off 6 (7, 7) stitches, purl to end.
3: KNIT ROW: Knit.
4: PURL ROW: Purl.
5: KNIT ROW: Knit.
6: PURL ROW: Purl.
7: KNIT ROW: Knit.
8: PURL ROW: Purl.
9: KNIT ROW: PURL this row.
10: PURL ROW: Purl
11: KNIT ROW: Knit.
12: PURL ROW: Purl.
13: KNIT ROW: Knit.
14: PURL ROW: Purl.
15: KNIT ROW: Knit.
16: PURL ROW: Purl.
17: KNIT ROW: Knit.
18: PURL ROW: Purl.
19: KNIT ROW: Knit.
Bind off loosely.

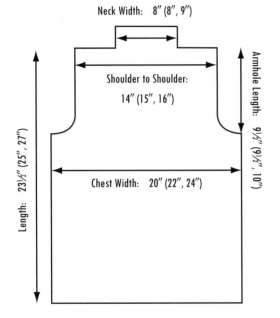

Neck Width: 8″ (8″, 9″)

Shoulder to Shoulder: 14″ (15″, 16″)

Armhole Length: 9½″ (9½″, 10″)

Length: 23½″ (25″, 27″)

Chest Width: 20″ (22″, 24″)

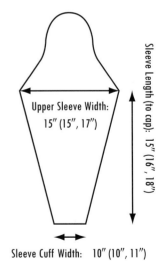

Upper Sleeve Width: 15″ (15″, 17″)

Sleeve Length (to cap): 15″ (16″, 18″)

Sleeve Cuff Width: 10″ (10″, 11″)

a tempting turtleneck

Allison took a beginner knitting class at our store.
She mastered knitting, purling, and ribbing very quickly and was extremely excited at the prospect of picking out yarn to start a project. Allison saw this sweater and knew it was exactly what she wanted to make. It is a very versatile look that can be worn with jeans or a skirt or a nice pair of pants. The fact that there was no neck shaping was a plus and Allison thought that the big ribbings on the cuffs, the bottom, and the turtleneck were great details. Sometimes a ribbing like this can be tough for a beginner, but with a little perseverance Allison got through the ribbing and cruised on the rest of the sweater.

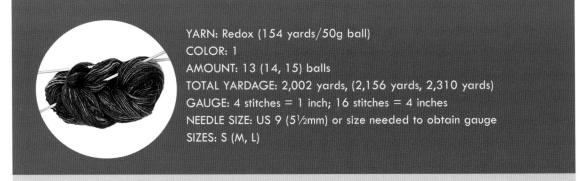

YARN: Redox (154 yards/50g ball)
COLOR: 1
AMOUNT: 13 (14, 15) balls
TOTAL YARDAGE: 2,002 yards, (2,156 yards, 2,310 yards)
GAUGE: 4 stitches = 1 inch; 16 stitches = 4 inches
NEEDLE SIZE: US 9 (5½mm) or size needed to obtain gauge
SIZES: S (M, L)

- Yarn is worked doubled throughout the sweater—this means you should hold 2 strands of yarn together as though they are 1.
- This pattern requires an edge stitch—this means you must always knit (K) the first and the last stitch.

back and front (make 2):

With #9 needle and 2 strands of yarn, cast on 78 (86, 90) stitches. Work K4, P4 ribbing as follows: For Small & Medium: Row 1: K1 edge stitch, K4 *(P4, K4)* to end, K1 edge stitch. Row 2: K1 edge stitch, P4 *(K4, P4)* to end, K1 edge stitch. Repeat rows 1 & 2 until piece measures 5″. For Large: Rows 1 & 2: K1 edge stitch, *K4, P4* to end, K1 edge stitch. Repeat rows 1 & 2 until piece measures 5″. For all sizes, continue in St st until piece measures 14½″ (16″, 16½″) from cast-on edge, ending with a WS row. **SHAPE ARMHOLES:** Bind off 4 stitches at the beginning of the next 2 rows. Bind off 3 stitches at the beginning of the next 2 rows. Bind off 2 stitches at the beginning of the next 2 rows. Then decrease 1 stitch at each edge every other row 5 (6, 5) times until 50 (56, 62) stitches remain. Continue to work in St st until piece measures 23½″ (25″, 26″) from cast-on edge. **SHAPE FUNNEL NECK:** Bind off 10 (12, 15) stitches at the beginning of the next 2 rows. Work K4, P4 ribbing for 6″.

Bind off remaining 30 (32, 32) stitches.

sleeves (make 2):

With #9 needle and 2 strands of yarn, cast on 38 (38, 42) stitches. For Small & Medium: Row 1: K1 edge stitch, K4 *(P4, K4)* to end, K1 edge stitch. Row 2: K1 edge stitch, P4 *(K4, P4)* to end, K1 edge stitch. Repeat rows 1 & 2 until piece measures 5″. For Large: Rows 1 & 2: K1 edge stitch, *K4, P4* to end, K1 edge stitch. Repeat rows 1 & 2 until piece measures 5″. For all sizes, continue in St st. At the same time, increase 1 stitch at each edge every 6th row 10 (11, 11) times until you have 58 (60, 64) stitches. Continue in St st until sleeve measures 17½″ (19″, 20″). **NOTE:** Increase leaving 2 edge stitches on either side of work. This means you should knit 2 stitches, increase a stitch, knit to the last 2 stitches, increase a stitch, and then knit the remaining 2 stitches. Increasing like this makes it easier to sew up your seams. **SHAPE CAP:** Bind off 4 stitches at the beginning of the next 2 rows. Bind off 3 stitches at the beginning of the next 2 rows. Bind off 2 stitches at the beginning of the next 2 rows. Then bind off 1 stitch at the beginning of the next 28 (30, 32) rows. Bind off remaining 12 (12, 14) stitches.

finishing:

Sew shoulder seams together. Sew sleeves on. Sew side and sleeve seams.

STEP-BY-STEP GUIDE TO SHAPING THE ARMHOLE

1: KNIT ROW: Bind off 4 stitches, knit to end.
2: PURL ROW: Bind off 4 stitches, purl to end.
3: KNIT ROW: Bind off 3 stitches, knit to end.
4: PURL ROW: Bind off 3 stitches, purl to end.
5: KNIT ROW: Bind off 2 stitches, knit to end.
6: PURL ROW: Bind off 2 stitches, purl to end.
7: KNIT ROW: Knit 1 stitch, K2tog, knit until 3 stitches remain on left needle, K2tog, K1.
8: PURL ROW: Purl.
Repeat rows 7 & 8 4 (5, 4) more times.

STEP-BY-STEP GUIDE TO SHAPING THE FUNNEL NECK

1: KNIT ROW: Bind off 10 (12, 15) stitches, knit to end.
2: PURL ROW: Bind off 10 (12, 15) stitches, purl to end.

For Small
3: RIGHT SIDE ROW: K1* (K4, P4)* K1
4: WRONG SIDE ROW: K1* (K4, P4)* K1
Repeat rows 3 & 4 for 6".
Bind off loosely.

For Medium and Large
3: RIGHT SIDE ROW: K4, P4.
4: WRONG SIDE ROW: K4, P4.
Repeat rows 3 & 4 for 6".
Bind off loosely.

Neck Width: 7½" (8", 8")

Shoulder to Shoulder: 12½" (14", 15½")

Armhole Length: 9" (9", 9¼")

Length: 23½" (25", 27")

Chest Width: 19½" (21½", 22½")

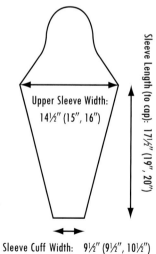

Sleeve Length (to cap): 17½" (19", 20")

Upper Sleeve Width: 14½" (15", 16")

Sleeve Cuff Width: 9½" (9½", 10½")

funky funnel-neck fun

Say it ten times fast. Funky Funnel-Neck Fun, Funky Funnel-Neck Fun, Funky Funnel-Neck Fun, Funky Funnel-Neck Fun, Funky Funnel-Neck Fun, Funky Funnel-Neck Fun, Funky Funnel-Neck Fun, Funky Funnel-Neck Fun, Funky Funnel-Neck Fun, Funky Funnel-Neck Fun.

You'll have completed this sweater before you master this tongue twister!

YARN: Polar (60 yards/50g ball)
COLOR: #70
AMOUNT: 12 (13, 14) balls
TOTAL YARDAGE: 720 yards, (780 yards, 840 yards)
GAUGE: 3 stitches = 1 inch; 12 stitches = 4 inches
NEEDLE SIZE: US 10½ (7mm) or size needed to obtain gauge
SIZES: S (M, L)

back and front (make 2):

With #10½ needle cast on 60 (66, 72) stitches. Work in St st until piece measures 15″ (16″, 17″) from cast-on edge, ending with a WS row. **SHAPE ARMHOLES:** Bind off 4 stitches at the beginning of the next 2 rows. Bind off 3 stitches at the beginning of the next 2 rows. Bind off 2 stitches at the beginning of the next 2 rows. Then decrease 1 stitch at each edge every other row 1 (2, 4) times until 40 (44, 46) stitches remain. Continue to work in St st until piece measures 23½″ (25″, 26″) from cast-on edge, ending with a WS row. **FUNNEL NECK:** Bind off 8 (10, 10) stitches at the beginning of the next 2 rows. Continue to work in St st for 2½″. Bind off remaining 24 (24, 26) stitches.

sleeves (make 2):

With #10½ needle, cast on 30 (30, 32) stitches. Work in St st. At the same time, increase 1 stitch at each edge every 8th row 7 times until you have 44 (44, 46) stitches. Continue in St st until sleeve measures 19″ (20″, 22″). **NOTE:** Increase leaving 2 edge stitches on either side of work. This means you should knit 2 stitches, increase a stitch, knit to the last 2 stitches, increase a stitch, and then knit the remaining 2 stitches. Increasing like this makes it easier to sew up your seams. **SHAPE CAP:** Bind off 4 stitches at the beginning of the next 2 rows. Bind off 3 stitches at the beginning of the next 2 rows. Bind off 2 stitches at the beginning of the next 2 rows. Then bind off 1 stitch at the beginning of the next 18 (18, 20) rows. Bind off remaining 8 stitches.

finishing:

Sew shoulder seams together. Sew sleeves on. Sew side and sleeve seams.

1: KNIT ROW: Bind off 4 stitches, knit to end.
2: PURL ROW: Bind off 4 stitches, purl to end.
3: KNIT ROW: Bind off 3 stitches, knit to end.
4: PURL ROW: Bind off 3 stitches, purl to end.
5: KNIT ROW: Bind off 2 stitches, knit to end.
6: PURL ROW: Bind off 2 stitches, purl to end.
7: KNIT ROW: Knit 1 stitch, K2tog, knit until 3 stitches remain on left needle, K2tog, K1.
8: PURL ROW: Purl.
   Repeat rows 7 & 8 0 (1, 3) more times.

1: KNIT ROW: Bind off 8 (10,10) stitches, knit to end.
2: PURL ROW: Bind off 8 (10,10) stitches, purl to end.
3: KNIT ROW: Knit.
4: PURL ROW: Purl.
   Repeat rows 3 & 4 for 2½".
   Bind off loosely.

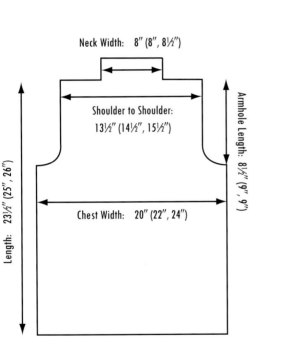

Neck Width: 8" (8", 8½")

Shoulder to Shoulder: 13½" (14½", 15½")

Armhole Length: 8½" (9", 9")

Chest Width: 20" (22", 24")

Length: 23½" (25", 26")

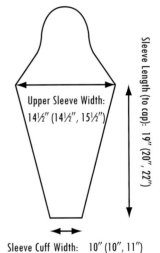

Sleeve Length (to cap): 19" (20", 22")

Upper Sleeve Width: 14½" (14½", 15½")

Sleeve Cuff Width: 10" (10", 11")

Crewneck Pullovers

Crewneck pullovers are probably the most popular and basic sweater shape. They encompass mock turtlenecks and turtlenecks too. The difference is simply in how many inches you knit after picking up for the neck. Crewnecks are very simple to make. Really, the only tricky part is shaping the neck on the front of the sweater (there is no shaping on the back; you just bind off straight across). If you follow our step-by-step directions, work one side of the neck at a time, and remember that you always bind off *going away from* the neck, you shouldn't have any problems.

Weekend Warrior is great because it has no ribbing on the bottom or cuffs. The yarn is so thick, it hangs straight instead of rolling at the edges even without the ribbing. *Don't Be a Football Widow* presents a little more challenge because it has a big ribbing on the bottom and a great big turtleneck. But don't let that put you off—it is knit on such jumbo needles, the ribbings knit up in no time and before you know it you're back to good old stockinette stitch. *Trick or Treat* is similar to *Don't Be a Football Widow* in that it has ribbings on all edges, but it has a mock turtleneck instead of a turtleneck. What's the difference? For a mock turtleneck you rib for 3", for a turtleneck you rib for 7"–8". You can interchange any of these necks. Knit more on one to make a turtleneck, or less on another to make a crew neck or a mock turtleneck.

don't be a football widow

Dana's husband, Jeff, was a rabid sports fan who was glued to the television every Sunday afternoon. Dana complained constantly to her sister, Jessie, about this predicament, so Jessie signed Dana up for a knitting class at our store, figuring that knitting was something Dana could do while Jeff was planted in front of the TV.

Dana loved the idea so much, she gave the first sweater she made to Jessie, who has been wearing it ever since. This sweater is a great first project because it is knitted on size 19 needles (almost as big as they come) and goes superfast. Now Jeff is hoping his team makes it to the playoffs so Dana will have time to make one for him; he claims that he deserves one because if he wasn't such a big football fan, she never would have learned to knit.

YARN: Horstia Morroko (88 yards/200g ball)

COLOR: S13

AMOUNT: 5 (6, 7) balls

TOTAL YARDAGE: 440 yards (528 yards, 616 yards)

GAUGE: 1⅗ stitches = 1 inch; 8 stitches = 5 inches

NEEDLE SIZE: US 15 (10mm) for ribbing, US 19 (15mm) for body, or sizes needed to obtain gauge

SIZES: S (M, L)

This pattern requires an edge stitch—this means you must always knit the first and last stitch of every row.

back:

With #15 needle cast on 29 (32, 35) stitches. Work in K3, P3 ribbing as follows: For Small & Large: Row 1: K1 edge stitch, K3 *(P3, K3)* to end, K1 edge stitch. Row 2: K1 edge stitch, P3 *(K3, P3)* to end, K1 edge stitch. Repeat rows 1 & 2 for 3½". For Medium: Rows 1 & 2: K1 edge stitch, *K3, P3* to end, K1 edge stitch. Repeat rows 1 & 2 for 3½". For all sizes, continue on #19 needles in St st until piece measures 12" (13", 15½") from cast-on edge, ending with a WS row. **SHAPE ARMHOLES:** Bind off 2 stitches at the beginning of the next 2 rows. Then decrease 1 stitch at each edge every other row 2 (3, 3) times until 21 (22, 25) stitches remain. Continue to work in St st until piece measures 20½" (22", 25") from cast-on edge. Bind off remaining stitches.

front:

Work as for back until piece measures 12" (13", 15½"). **SHAPE ARMHOLES AS FOR BACK.** When piece measures 18" (19½", 22") from cast-on edge, ending with a WS row: **SHAPE**

CREWNECK: Bind off center 7 (8, 7) stitches. Working each side of neck separately, at the beginning of each neck edge every other row, bind off 2 stitches 1 time, 1 stitch 1 time until 4 (4, 6) stitches remain. Continue working on remaining stitches until piece measures 20½" (22", 25"). Bind off remaining stitches.

sleeves:

With #15 needle, cast on 14 (17, 20) stitches. Work in K3, P3 ribbing as follows: For Small & Large: Rows 1 & 2: K1 edge stitch, *K3, P3* to end, K1 edge stitch. Repeat rows 1 & 2 for 3½". For all sizes, continue in St st and at the same time, increase 1 stitch at each edge every 6th row 5 times until 24 (27, 30). For Medium: Row 1: K1 edge stitch, K3 *(P3, K3)* to end, K1 edge stitch. Row 2: K1 edge stitch, P3 *(K3, P3)* to end, K1 edge stitch. Repeat rows 1 & 2 for 3½". Continue in St st until sleeve measures 15½" (16½", 17½"). **NOTE:** Increase leaving 2 edge stitches on either side of work. This means you should knit 2 stitches, increase a stitch, knit to the last 2 stitches, increase a stitch, and then knit the remaining 2 stitches. Increasing like this makes it easier to sew up your seams.

SHAPE CAP: Bind off 2 stitches at the beginning of the next 2 rows. Then decrease 1 stitch at each edge every other row 2 (3, 4) times. Bind off 1 stitch at beginning of the next 8 rows. Bind off remaining 8 (9, 10) stitches.

finishing:

Sew shoulder seams together. Sew sleeves on. Sew side and sleeve seams. With #15 16-inch circular needle, pick up 30 (36, 36) stitches and work in K3, P3 ribbing for 8″. Bind off loosely.

STEP-BY-STEP GUIDE TO SHAPING THE ARMHOLE

1: KNIT ROW: Bind off 2 stitches, knit to end.
2: PURL ROW: Bind off 2 stitches, purl to end.
3: KNIT ROW: Knit 1 stitch, K2tog, knit until 3 stitches remain on left needle, K2tog, K1.
4: PURL ROW: Purl.
   Repeat rows 3 & 4 1 (2, 2) more times.

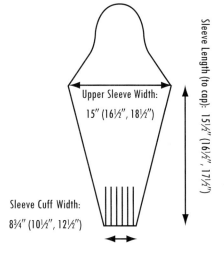

Upper Sleeve Width: 15″ (16½″, 18½″)

Sleeve Cuff Width: 8¾″ (10½″, 12½″)

Sleeve Length (to cap): 15½″ (16½″, 17½″)

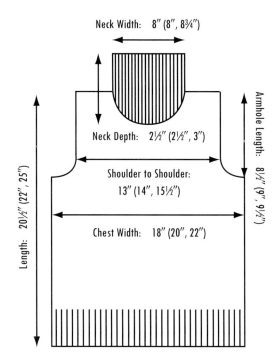

Neck Width: 8″ (8″, 8¾″)

Neck Depth: 2½″ (2½″, 3″)

Armhole Length: 8½″ (9″, 9½″)

Shoulder to Shoulder: 13″ (14″, 15½″)

Chest Width: 18″ (20″, 22″)

Length: 20½″ (22″, 25″)

Remember that after binding off the center stitches, you will work one side of the neck at a time.

1: KNIT ROW: Knit 9 (9,10) stitches; with the 8th (8th, 9th) stitch begin to bind off the center 7 (8, 7) stitches. For example, for size Small this means you should pull the 8th stitch over the 9th stitch and this is your first bind off. When you are done binding off the center 7 (8, 7) stitches, check to make sure you have 7 (7, 9) stitches on each side of the hole including the stitch on the right needle. Knit to end of row. Turn work.

2: PURL ROW: Purl 1 row. Turn work.

3: KNIT ROW: Bind off first 2 stitches. Knit to end of row. Turn work.

4: PURL ROW: Purl 1 row. Turn work.

5: KNIT ROW: Bind off 1 stitch. Knit to end of row. Turn work.

6: PURL ROW: Purl 1 row. Turn work.

- When you are done with the bind-off instructions, measure the length of the front piece, comparing it to the length of the back. If the front and back measure the same, bind off the remaining stitches. If the front is too short, continue knitting and purling until the pieces are of equal length, then bind off.

- Attach yarn to the remaining stitches on the other side of the neck edge and begin binding off 2 stitches immediately. You will now be binding off when you are purling. Finish neck shaping as for the other side and bind off.

the weekend warrior

You can't imagine how many people come into our store and tell us that they need to knit a sweater *fast and* it must be easy and of course beautiful. Carrie was one of them. She had only a few days to make a sweater for her sister's birthday and, although she had just recently learned to knit, she had her heart set on a hand-knitted gift. She saw this sweater and figured she could fly through the project since it's on #17 needles and all that's required is knitting and purling. She was right. She bought the yarn on Thursday and was done by Sunday evening. She even went on a date on Saturday night!

YARN: Colinette Point Five (55 yards/100g ball)
COLOR: Dark Umber
AMOUNT: 8 (9, 9) balls
TOTAL YARDAGE: 440 yards (495 yards, 495 yards)
GAUGE: 2¼ stitches = 1 inch; 9 stitches = 4 inches
NEEDLE SIZE: US 17 (12mm) or size needed to obtain gauge
SIZES: S (M, L)

back:

With #17 needle, cast on 44 (48, 52) stitches. Work in St st until piece measures 15½" (16", 16½") from cast-on edge, ending with a WS row. **SHAPE ARMHOLES:** Bind off 3 stitches at the beginning of the next 2 rows. Then decrease 1 stitch at each edge every other row 4 (5, 6) times until 30 (32, 34) stitches remain. Continue to work in St st until piece measures 24" (25", 26") from cast-on edge. Bind off remaining stitches.

front:

Work as for back until piece measures 15½" (16", 16½"). **SHAPE ARMHOLES AS FOR BACK.** Continue to work in St st until piece measures 21½" (22½", 23½"), ending with a WS row. **SHAPE CREWNECK:** Bind off center 8 stitches. Working each side of neck separately, at the beginning of each neck edge every other row, bind off 2 stitches 1 time, 1 stitch 2 (3, 3) times. Work on remaining 7 (7, 8) stitches until piece measures 24" (25", 26"). Bind off remaining stitches.

sleeves:

With #17 needle, cast on 18 (20, 22) stitches. Work in St st. At the same time, increase one stitch at each edge every 8th row 4 (2, 2) times until you have 26 (24, 26 sts) then every 6th row 3 (6, 6) times until you have 32 (36, 38) stitches. Continue in St st until sleeve measures 19" (20", 22").
NOTE: Increase leaving 2 edge stitches on either side of work. This means you should knit 2 stitches, increase a stitch, knit to the last 2 stitches, increase a stitch, and then knit the remaining 2 stitches. Increasing like this makes it easier to sew up your seams.
SHAPE CAP: Bind off 3 stitches at the beginning of the next 2 rows. Then decrease 1 stitch at each end every other row 4 (3, 4) times. Bind off remaining 18 (24, 24) stitches.

finishing:

Sew shoulder seams together. Sew sleeves on. Sew side and sleeve seams. With 16-inch #15 circular needle, pick up 36 (36, 40) stitches around the neck. Work in K2, P2 ribbing for 4 rows. Bind off loosely.

1: KNIT ROW: Bind off 3 stitches, knit to end.
2: PURL ROW: Bind off 3 stitches, purl to end.
3: KNIT ROW: Knit 1 stitch, K2tog, knit until 3 stitches remain on left needle, K2tog, K1.
4: PURL ROW: Purl.
   Repeat rows 3 & 4 3 (4, 5) more times.

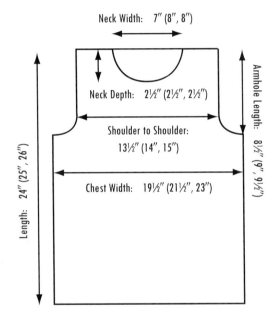

Neck Width: 7" (8", 8")

Neck Depth: 2½" (2½", 2½")

Shoulder to Shoulder: 13½" (14", 15")

Chest Width: 19½" (21½", 23")

Armhole Length: 8½" (9", 9½")

Length: 24" (25", 26")

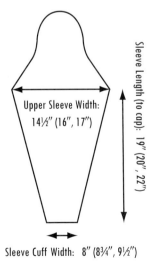

Upper Sleeve Width: 14½" (16", 17")

Sleeve Length (to cap): 19" (20", 22")

Sleeve Cuff Width: 8" (8¾", 9½")

Remember that after binding off the center stitches, you will work one side of the neck at a time.

1: KNIT ROW: Knit 13 (14, 15) stitches; with the 12th (13th, 14th) stitch, begin to bind off the center 8 stitches. For example, for size Small, this means you should pull the 12th stitch over the 13th stitch and this is your first bind off. When you are done binding off the center 8 stitches, check to make sure you have 11 (12, 13) stitches on each side of the hole including the stitch on the right needle. Knit to end of row. Turn work.
2: PURL ROW: Purl 1 row. Turn work.
3: KNIT ROW: Bind off first 2 stitches. Knit to end of row. Turn work.
4: PURL ROW: Purl 1 row. Turn work.
5: KNIT ROW: Bind off 1 stitch. Knit to end of row. Turn work.
6: PURL ROW: Purl 1 row. Turn work.
   Repeat rows 5 & 6 1 (2, 2) more times.

- When you are done with the bind-off instructions, measure the length of the front piece, comparing it to the length of the back. If the front and back measure the same, bind off the remaining stitches. If the front is too short, continue knitting and purling until the pieces are of equal length, and bind off.

- Attach yarn to the remaining stitches on the other side of the neck edge and begin binding off 2 stitches immediately. You will now be binding off when you are purling. Finish neck shaping as for the other side and bind off.

trick or treat

We sort of tricked Jane into making this sweater. She already knew how to knit and purl when we met her, but she wasn't confident enough in her skills to attempt an actual garment. After watching her knit for a while, we knew she was up to it, even if she didn't, so we started her on a scarf that was knit in stockinette stitch and wide enough that it wouldn't matter if the scarf rolled in a bit at the edges. We told her to come back so we could check her work after twelve inches. Tricky us. Sure enough, three days and twelve easy inches later she was regretting not having tackled something more ambitious. Imagine her surprise when we did some minor adjusting and changed the scarf . . . into a sweater.

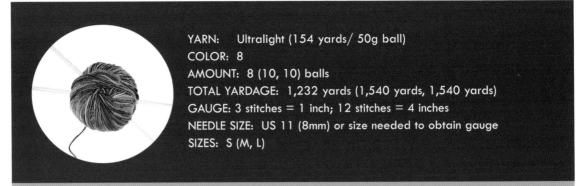

YARN: Ultralight (154 yards/ 50g ball)
COLOR: 8
AMOUNT: 8 (10, 10) balls
TOTAL YARDAGE: 1,232 yards (1,540 yards, 1,540 yards)
GAUGE: 3 stitches = 1 inch; 12 stitches = 4 inches
NEEDLE SIZE: US 11 (8mm) or size needed to obtain gauge
SIZES: S (M, L)

- Yarn is worked doubled throughout the sweater—this means you should hold 2 strands of yarn together as though they are 1.
- This pattern requires an edge stitch—this means you must always knit the first and the last stitch.

back:

With #11 needle and 2 strands of yarn, cast on 58 (66, 74) stitches. Work in K4, P4 ribbing as follows: K1 edge stitch, *K4, P4* to end, K1 edge stitch. Work in ribbing for 4″. Then work in St st until piece measures 12″ (13½″, 16″) from cast-on edge, ending with a WS row. **SHAPE ARMHOLES:** Bind off 3 stitches at the beginning of the next 2 rows. Bind off 2 stitches at the beginning of the following 2 rows. Then decrease 1 stitch at each edge every other row 2 (4, 6) times, until 44 (48, 52) stitches remain. Continue to work in St st until piece measures 20″ (22″, 25″) from cast-on edge. Bind off remaining stitches.

front:

Work as for back until piece measures 12″ (13½″, 16″). **SHAPE ARMHOLES AS FOR BACK.** Continue in St st until piece measures 17½″ (19½″, 22½″) from cast-on edge, ending with a WS row. **SHAPE CREWNECK:** Bind off center 6 stitches. Working each side of neck separately, at the beginning of each neck edge every other row, bind off 3 stitches 1 time, 2 stitches 2 times, 1 stitch 1 (2, 2) times. Continue working in St st on remaining 11 (12, 14) stitches until piece

measures 20″ (22″, 25″) from cast-on edge. Bind off remaining stitches.

sleeves:

With #11 needle and 2 strands of yarn, cast on 26 (26, 30) stitches. Work in K4, P4 ribbing as follows: For Small & Medium: Rows 1 & 2: K1 edge stitch, *K4, P4* to end, K1 edge stitch. Repeat rows 1 & 2 for 2″. For Large: Row 1: K1 edge stitch, K4 *(P4, K4)* to end, K1 edge stitch. Row 2: K1 edge stitch, P4 *(K4, P4)* to end, K1 edge stitch. Repeat rows 1 & 2 until piece measures 2″. Continue in St st. At the same time, increase 1 stitch at each edge every 6th row 10 (11, 11) times until you have 46 (48, 52) stitches. Continue in St st until sleeve measures 16″ (17″, 18″). **NOTE:** Increase leaving 2 edge stitches on either side of work. This means you should knit 2 stitches, increase a stitch, knit to the last 2 stitches, increase a stitch, and then knit the remaining 2 stitches. Increasing like this makes it easier to sew up your seams. **SHAPE CAP:** Bind off 3 stitches at the beginning of the next 2 rows. Bind off 2 stitches at the beginning of the next 16 (16, 18) rows. Bind off remaining 8 (10, 10) stitches.

finishing:

Sew shoulder seams together. Sew sleeves on. Sew up side and sleeve seams. With #11 16-inch circular needle, pick up 48 stitches around neck and work in K4, P4 ribbing for 2". Bind off loosely.

STEP-BY-STEP GUIDE TO SHAPING THE ARMHOLE

1: KNIT ROW: Bind off 3 stitches, knit to end.
2: PURL ROW: Bind off 3 stitches, purl to end.
3: KNIT ROW: Bind off 2 stitches, knit to end.
4: PURL ROW: Bind off 2 stitches, purl to end.
5: KNIT ROW: Knit 1 stitch, K2tog, knit until 3 stitches remain on left needle, K2tog, K1.
6: PURL ROW: Purl.
    Repeat rows 5 & 6 1 (3, 5) more times.

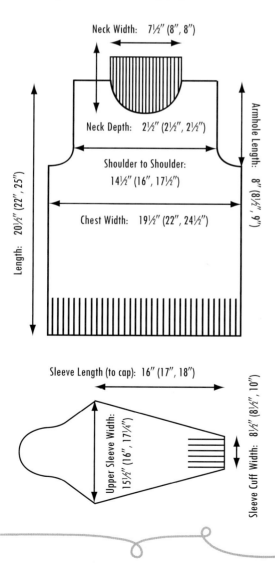

STEP-BY-STEP GUIDE TO SHAPING THE CREWNECK

Remember that after binding off the center stitches, you will work one side of the neck at a time.

1: KNIT ROW: Knit 21(23, 25) stitches; with the 20th (22nd, 24th) stitch begin to bind off the center 6 stitches. For example, for size Small, this means you should pull the 20th stitch over the 21st stitch and this is your first bind off. When you are done binding off the center 6 stitches, check to make sure you have 19 (21, 23) stitches on each side of the hole including the stitch on the right needle. Knit to end of row. Turn work.
2: PURL ROW: Purl 1 row. Turn work.
3: KNIT ROW: Bind off first 3 stitches. Knit to end of row. Turn work.
4: PURL ROW: Purl 1 row. Turn work.
5: KNIT ROW: Bind off first 2 stitches. Knit to end of row. Turn work.
6: PURL ROW: Purl 1 row. Turn work.
7: KNIT ROW: Bind off first 2 stitches. Knit to end of row. Turn work.
8: PURL ROW: Purl 1 row. Turn work.
9: KNIT ROW: Bind off 1 stitch. Knit to end of row. Turn work.
10: PURL ROW: Purl 1 row. Turn work.
    Repeat rows 9 & 10 0 (1, 1) more times.

• When you are done with the bind-off instructions, measure the length of the front piece, comparing it to the length of the back. If the front and back measure the same, bind off the remaining stitches. If the front is too short, continue knitting and purling until the pieces are of equal length, then bind off.

• Attach yarn to the remaining stitches on the other side of the neck edge and begin binding off 3 stitches immediately. You will now be binding off when you are purling. Finish neck shaping as for the other side and bind off.

Cardigans

Our customers are always surprised to learn that cardigans are just as easy to knit as pullover sweaters. The back and sleeve directions mimic those of a pullover and the front is just split in half and knit in two separate pieces. The most important thing to remember when making a cardigan is to be sure to shape the armhole on one side of each front and the neck on the opposite side. If you follow our step-by-step instructions you won't have any problems. Really, the only aspect of knitting a cardigan that is a little bit challenging is the finishing; you have to pick up stitches for button bands and make buttonholes. Picking up stitches for bands is no harder than doing so for a neck, and buttonholes are just a simple combination of yarn overs and decreases.

The cardigans in this book all vary slightly. *The Problem Solver* is an extremely simple cardigan, but it has a V-neck. It uses a crochet edging as a border instead of ribbing and doesn't require any buttonholes since we put in a zipper. *Give the People What They Want* is the most advanced of the three, but it's still pretty simple and straightforward, with big ribbing, cuffs, a collar, and slits at the sides. *A Craving to Knit* is as basic as it gets, with a crewneck and small ribbing at the edges. If you want to add cuffs or a collar, check to see how we achieved the look on *Give the People What They Want* and just knit your rib longer. If you want slits, don't sew your side seams all the way down. See how easy?

the problem solver

Lily bought a great pair of pants. She liked everything about them. They were a unique color, brown with a hint of purple but not quite eggplant. Best of all they fit her perfectly, and she couldn't wait to wear them. When she got home, however, she found that she didn't like the way any of her shirts or sweaters looked with them. Lily stopped into our shop on her way to return the pants and told us her tale of woe. No way, we said. We scoured the store for a perfect color match until we found this combination of yarns, which picked up all the subtle shades in her pants perfectly. Problem solved!

This sweater will solve a multitude of problems for you too. It offers a great opportunity for mixing and matching colors and textures and is the perfect shape to wear with your favorite pair of jeans or a hot new suede skirt.

YARN: Crystal Palace Chenille (100 yd/50g skein) & Classic Elite Fame (116 yd/50g skein)

COLOR: Chenille Color 5800; Fame Color 1407

AMOUNT: 8 (10, 12) balls Fame; 6 (7, 9) balls Chenille

TOTAL YARDAGE: 1,392 (1,740, 1,972) yards Fame; 600 (700, 900) yards Chenille

GAUGE: 2½ stitches = 1 inch; 10 stitches = 4 inches

NEEDLE SIZE: US 13 (9mm) or size needed to obtain gauge

SIZES: S (M, L)

Yarn is worked tripled throughout the sweater—this means you should hold 1 strand of Chenille and 2 strands of Fame together as though they are 1.

back:

With #13 needle and 3 strands of yarn, cast on 44 (48, 52) stitches. Work in St st until piece measures 12″ (13½″, 15″) from cast-on edge, ending with a WS row. **SHAPE ARMHOLES:** Bind off 3 stitches at the beginning of the next 2 rows. Then decrease 1 stitch at each edge every other row 3 (3, 4) times until 32 (36, 38) stitches remain. Continue to work in St st until piece measures 20″ (22″, 24″) from cast-on edge. Bind off remaining stitches.

front: (make 2, reversing shaping)

With #13 needle and 3 strands of yarn, cast on 22 (24, 26) stitches. Work in St st until piece measures 12″ (13½″, 15″) from cast-on edge, ending with a WS row. **SHAPE ARMHOLE AS FOR BACK.** (Remember that you are shaping the armhole on only 1 side of each front.) 16 (18,19) stitches remain. Continue to work in St st until piece measures 13″ (15″, 17″) from cast-on edge ending with a WS row. **SHAPE NECK:** *For left front (when worn):* Row 1: Knit to last 4 stitches, K2tog, K2. Row 2: Purl. Repeat rows 1 & 2 6 (7, 8) more times. 9 (10, 10) stitches remain. When the piece measures the same as the back, bind off remaining stitches. *For right front (when worn):* Row 1: K2, SSK, knit to end. Row 2: Purl. Repeats rows 1 & 2 6 (7, 8) more times. 9 (10, 10) stitches remain. When the piece measures the same as the back, bind off remaining stitches. **NOTE:** It is very likely that you will have to shape both the neck and the armhole at the same time on the fronts of the V-neck cardigan. You must begin shaping each at the designated length.

sleeves:

With #13 needle and 3 strands of yarn, cast on 20 (22, 22) stitches. Work in St st. At the same time, increase 1 stitch at each edge every 8th (8th, 6th) row 8 (8, 10) times until you have 36 (38, 42) stitches. Continue in St st until sleeve measures 18″ (19″, 20″). **NOTE:** Increase leaving 2 edge stitches on either side of work. This means you should knit 2 stitches, increase a stitch, knit to the last 2 stitches, increase a stitch, and then knit the remaining 2 stitches. Increasing like this makes it easier to sew up your seams. **SHAPE CAP:** Bind off 3 stitches at the beginning of the next 2 rows.

Then decrease 1 stitch at each end every other row 3 (3, 4) times. Bind off remaining 3 stitches at beginning of next 6 rows. Bind off remaining 6 (8, 10) stitches.

finishing:

Sew shoulder seams together. Sew sleeves on. Sew side and sleeve seams. With size K (7½mm) crochet hook, do 1 row of single-crochet and 1 row of shrimp-stitch around all edges. Have a tailor put in a zipper or purchase a zipper that measures the length from the bottom of your sweater to the beginning of the V-neck and insert it your-self, following the directions on the package and using thread in a matching color.

STEP-BY-STEP GUIDE TO SHAPING THE ARMHOLE

BACK
1: KNIT ROW: Bind off 3 stitches, knit to end.
2: PURL ROW: Bind off 3 stitches, purl to end.
3: KNIT ROW: Knit 1 stitch, K2tog, knit until 3 stitches remain on left needle, K2tog, K1.
4: PURL ROW: Purl.
   Repeat rows 3 & 4 2 (2, 3) more times.

LEFT FRONT (left side when worn)
1: KNIT ROW: Bind off 3 stitches, knit to end.
2: PURL ROW: Purl.
3: KNIT ROW: Knit 1 stitch, K2tog, knit to end.
4: PURL ROW: Purl.
   Repeat rows 3 & 4 2 (2, 3) more times.

RIGHT FRONT (right side when worn)
1: PURL ROW: Bind off 3 stitches, purl to end.
2: KNIT ROW: Knit.
3: PURL ROW: Purl.
4: KNIT ROW: Knit to last 3 stitches, K2tog, K1.
   Repeat rows 3 & 4 2 (2, 3) more times.

STEP-BY-STEP GUIDE TO SHAPING THE V-NECK

LEFT FRONT (left side when worn)
1: KNIT ROW: Knit to last 4 stitches, K2tog, K2.
2: PURL ROW: Purl.
   Repeat rows 1 & 2 6 (7, 8) more times.

RIGHT FRONT (right side when worn)
1: KNIT ROW: K2, SSK, Knit to end of row.
2: PURL ROW: Purl.
   Repeat rows 1 & 2 6 (7, 8) more times.

• When you are done with the decrease instructions, measure the length of the front piece, comparing it to the back. If the front and back measure the same, bind off the remaining stitches. If the front is too short, continue knitting and purling until the pieces are of equal length, then bind off.

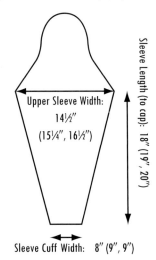

Upper Sleeve Width: 14½" (15¼", 16½")

Sleeve Length (to cap): 18" (19", 20")

Sleeve Cuff Width: 8" (9", 9")

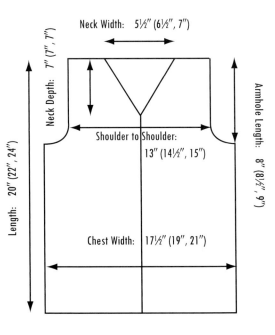

Neck Width: 5½" (6½", 7")

Neck Depth: 7" (7", 7")

Shoulder to Shoulder: 13" (14½", 15")

Armhole Length: 8" (8½", 9")

Length: 20" (22", 24")

Chest Width: 17½" (19", 21")

give the people what they want

This sweater is dedicated to all those customers who asked for a versatile, coatlike cardigan. "I want a sweater that can be used as a jacket at the office . . . or as a coat in the fall or spring." "I'd like to make a jacket with a collar; I'd like it to be casual but also be able to wear it if I'm going out at night." "I wish you had a pattern for a cardigan that I could wear as a light jacket, indoors or outdoors." Clearly, everyone needs at least one sweater like this. So, who are we to deny our customers what they want?

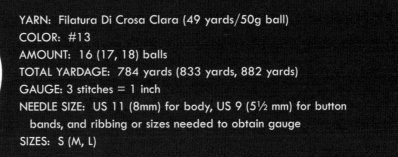

YARN: Filatura Di Crosa Clara (49 yards/50g ball)
COLOR: #13
AMOUNT: 16 (17, 18) balls
TOTAL YARDAGE: 784 yards (833 yards, 882 yards)
GAUGE: 3 stitches = 1 inch
NEEDLE SIZE: US 11 (8mm) for body, US 9 (5½ mm) for button
   bands, and ribbing or sizes needed to obtain gauge
SIZES: S (M, L)

back:

With #9 needle cast on 63 (66, 72) stitches. Work in K3, P3 ribbing as follows: For Small: Row 1: K3 *(P3, K3)* to end. Row 2: P3 *(K3, P3)* to end. Repeat rows 1 & 2 for 4". For Medium & Large: Rows 1 & 2: *K3, P3* to end. Repeat rows 1 & 2 for 4". Decrease 1 stitch on the last row of ribbing for Small only (62 stitches remain). Change to #11 needle and then work in St st until piece measures 16½" (17½", 18½") from cast-on edge, ending with a WS row. **SHAPE ARMHOLES:** Bind off 4 stitches at the beginning of the next 2 rows. Bind off 3 stitches at the beginning of the next 2 rows. Bind off 2 stitches at the beginning of the next 2 rows. Then decrease 1 stitch at each edge every other row 1 (2, 4) times until 42 (44, 46) stitches remain. Continue to work in St st until piece measures 25" (26", 27½") from cast-on edge. Bind off remaining stitches.

front: (make 2, reversing shaping)

With #9 needle, cast on 30 (33, 36) stitches. Work in K3, P3 ribbing as follows: For Small & Large: Rows 1 & 2 * K3, P3* to end. Repeat rows 1 & 2 for 4". For Medium: Row 1: K3 *(P3, K3)* to end. Row 2: P3 *(K3, P3)* to end. Repeat rows 1 & 2 for 4". Decrease 1 stitch on the last row of ribbing for Medium only (32

stitches remain). Change to #11 needle and then work in St st until piece measures 16½" (17½", 18½") from cast-on edge, ending with a WS row. **SHAPE ARMHOLE AS FOR BACK.** (Remember that you are shaping the armhole on only 1 side of each front.) 20 (21, 23) stitches remain. Continue to work in St st until piece measures 22" (23", 24½") from cast-on edge. **SHAPE CREWNECK:** At beginning of each neck edge every other row bind off 4 stitches 1 time, 3 stitches 1 time, 2 stitches 1 time, 1 stitch 1 (2, 3) times. When the piece measures the same as the back, bind off remaining 10 (10, 11) stitches.

sleeves:

With #9 needle, cast on 30 (33, 36) stitches. Work in K3, P3 ribbing as follows: For Small & Large: Rows 1 & 2: *K3, P3* to end. Repeat rows 1 & 2 for 4". Medium: Row 1: K3 *(P3, K3)* to end. Row 2: P3 *(K3, P3)* to end. Repeat rows 1 & 2 for 4". Decrease 1 stitch on the last row of ribbing for Medium (32 stitches remain). Change to #11 needle and then work in St st. At the same time, increase 1 stitch at each edge every 4th row 9 (9, 8) times until you have 48 (50, 52) stitches.

Continue in St st until sleeve measures 16" (17", 18"). **NOTE:** Increase leaving 2 edge stitches on either side of work. This means you should knit 2 stitches, increase a stitch, knit to the last 2 stitches, increase a stitch, and then knit the remaining 2 stitches. Increasing like this makes it easier to sew up your seams. **SHAPE CAP:** Bind off 4 stitches at the beginning of the next 2 rows. Bind off 3 stitches at the beginning of the next two rows. Bind off 2 stitches at the beginning of the next 2 rows. Then decrease 1 stitch at each end every other row 7 times. Bind off remaining 16 (18, 20) stitches.

finishing:

Sew shoulder seams together. Sew sleeves on. Sew side and sleeve seams. With #9 needle, pick up 84 (86, 90) stitches on left (as worn) front for button band. Work K3, P3 ribbing for 8 rows. Bind off loosely. Pick up 84 (86, 90) stitches on right (as worn) front for buttonhole band. For sizes small and large, work in K3, P3 ribbing for 3 rows. For size medium work Row 1 (and all odd rows): K3, P3; Row 2 (and all even rows except row 4, see below): P3, K3.

FOR ALL SIZES make buttonholes on Row 4 as follows:

 Small: Rib 3 *(YO, rib 2tog, rib 17)* 4 times, end rib 2tog, YO, rib 3

 Medium: Rib 2 *(YO, rib 2tog, rib 18)* 4 times, end rib 2tog, YO, rib 2

 Large: Rib 2 *(YO, rib 2tog, rib 19)* 4 times, end rib 2tog, YO, rib 2.

NOTE: On Row 5 when you are knitting over a YO (yarn over), knit the stitch through the back. If you are purling over YO (yarn over), purl as usual.

Rib 2 means K1, P1; Rib 3 means K1, P1, K1.

Buttonholes are made on 1 row only.

Buttonhole band is placed on right front (as worn) for women, and left front for men.

Repeat 4 times refers to the instructions within the parentheses().

With #9 needle, beginning at the halfway point of the buttonhole band, pick up 93 stitches around neck edge. Work in K3, P3 rib as follows: Row 1: K3 P3; Row 2: P3 K3; repeat rows 1 and 2 until collar measures 4". Bind off loosely.

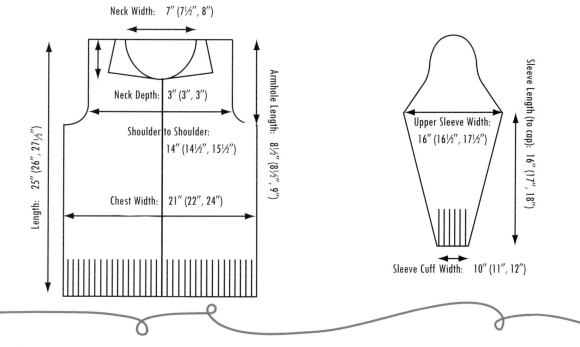

Neck Width: 7" (7½", 8")

Neck Depth: 3" (3", 3")

Shoulder to Shoulder: 14" (14½", 15½")

Chest Width: 21" (22", 24")

Length: 25" (26", 27½")

Armhole Length: 8½" (8½", 9")

Upper Sleeve Width: 16" (16½", 17½")

Sleeve Length (to cap): 16" (17", 18")

Sleeve Cuff Width: 10" (11", 12")

BACK

1: KNIT ROW: Bind off 4 stitches, knit to end.
2: PURL ROW: Bind off 4 stitches, purl to end.
3: KNIT ROW: Bind off 3 stitches, knit to end.
4: PURL ROW: Bind off 3 stitches, purl to end.
5: KNIT ROW: Bind off 2 stitches, knit to end.
6: PURL ROW: Bind off 2 stitches, purl to end.
7: KNIT ROW: Knit 1 stitch, K2tog, knit until 3 stitches remain on left needle, K2tog, K1.
8: PURL ROW: Purl.
Repeat rows 7 & 8 0 (1, 3) more times.

LEFT FRONT (left side when worn)

1: KNIT ROW: Bind off 4 stitches, knit to end.
2: PURL ROW: Purl.
3: KNIT ROW: Bind off 3 stitches, knit to end.
4: PURL ROW: Purl.
5: KNIT ROW: Bind off 2 stitches, knit to end.
6: PURL ROW: Purl.
7: KNIT ROW: Knit 1 stitch, K2tog, knit to end of row.
8: PURL ROW: Purl.
Repeat rows 7 & 8 0 (1, 3) more times.

RIGHT FRONT (right side when worn)

1: PURL ROW: Bind off 4 stitches, purl to end.
2: KNIT ROW: Knit.
3: PURL ROW: Bind off 3 stitches, purl to end.
4: KNIT ROW: Knit.
5: PURL ROW: Bind off 2 stitches, purl to end.
6: KNIT ROW: Knit to last 3 stitches, K2tog, K1.
7: PURL ROW: Purl.
Repeat rows 6 & 7 0 (1, 3) more times.

LEFT FRONT (left side when worn)

1: PURL ROW: Bind off 4 stitches, purl to end.
2: KNIT ROW: Knit.
3: PURL ROW: Bind off 3 stitches, purl to end.
4: KNIT ROW: Knit.
5: PURL ROW: Bind off 2 stitches, purl to end.
6: PURL ROW: Bind off 1 stitch, purl to end.
7: KNIT ROW: Knit.
Repeat rows 6 & 7 0 (1, 2) more times.

- When you are done with the decrease instructions, measure the length of the front piece, comparing it to the back. If the front and back measure the same, bind off the remaining stitches. If the front is too short, continue knitting and purling until the pieces are of equal length, then bind off.

RIGHT FRONT (right side when worn)

1: KNIT ROW: Bind off 4 stitches, knit to end.
2: PURL ROW: Purl.
3: KNIT ROW: Bind off 3 stitches, knit to end.
4: PURL ROW: Purl.
5: KNIT ROW: Bind off 2 stitches, knit to end.
6: PURL ROW: Purl.
7: KNIT ROW: Bind off 1 stitch, knit to end.
Repeat rows 6 & 7 0 (1, 2) more times.

- When you are done with the decrease instructions, measure the length of the front piece, comparing it to the back. If the front and back measure the same, bind off the remaining stitches. If the front is too short, continue knitting and purling until the pieces are of equal length, then bind off.

a craving to knit

When Susan, a good friend of ours from college, was in her sixth month of pregnancy, she found herself in the grip of a craving to knit even though she hadn't held a pair of needles since childhood. She knit a simple cardigan for her baby in a weekend, but her craving wasn't satisfied, so she decided to make this little number for herself. Now mommy and daughter have matching sweaters. How cute is that!

YARN: Adrienne Vittadini Sara (120 yards/50g ball)

COLOR: #1531

AMOUNT: 5 (6, 6) balls

TOTAL YARDAGE: 600 yards (720 yards, 720 yards)

GAUGE: 4 stitches = 1 inch; 16 stitches = 4 inches

NEEDLE SIZE: US 9 (5½ mm) or size needed to obtain gauge

SIZES: S (M, L)

back

With #9 needle, cast on 66 (76, 84) stitches. Work in K1, P1 ribbing for 1″. Then work in St st until piece measures 10½″ (12″, 13½″) from cast-on edge, ending with a WS row. **SHAPE ARMHOLES:** Bind off 3 (4, 4) stitches at the beginning of the next 2 rows. Bind off 3 stitches at the beginning of the next 0 (0, 2) rows. Bind off 2 stitches at the beginning of the next 4 (4, 2) rows. Then decrease 1 stitch at each edge every other row 2 (4, 4) times until 48 (52, 58) stitches remain. Continue to work in St st until piece measures 18″ (20″, 22″) from cast-on edge. Bind off remaining stitches.

front: (make 2, reverse shaping)

With #9 needle, cast on 34 (38, 42) stitches. Work in K1, P1 ribbing for 1″. Then work in St st until piece measures 10½″ (12″, 13½″) from cast-on edge, ending with a WS row. **SHAPE ARMHOLE AS FOR BACK** (Remember that you are shaping the armhole on only 1 side of each front) until 25, (26, 29) stitches remain. Continue to work in St st until piece measures 15½″ (17½″, 19½″) from cast-on edge. **SHAPE CREWNECK:** At beginning of each neck edge every other row bind off 4 stitches 1 time, 3 stitches 1 time, 2 stitches 1 time, 1 stitch 3 (3, 4) times. When the piece measures the same as the back, bind off remaining 13 (14, 16) stitches.

sleeves:

With #9 needle, cast on 32 (34, 36) stitches. Work in K1, P1 ribbing for 1″. Then work in St st. At the same time, increase 1 stitch at each edge every 6th row 13 times until you have 58 (60, 62) stitches. Continue in St st until sleeve measures 16″ (17″, 19″). **NOTE:** Increase leaving 2 edge stitches on either side of work. This means you should knit 2 stitches, increase a stitch, knit to the last 2 stitches, increase a stitch, and then knit the remaining 2 stitches. Increasing like this makes it easier to sew up your seams. **SHAPE CAP:** Bind off 3 (4, 4) stitches at the beginning of the next 2 rows. Bind off 3 stitches at the beginning of the next 0 (0, 2 rows). Bind off 2 stitches at the beginning of the next 4 (4, 2) rows. Then decrease 1 stitch at each end every other row 10 times. Bind off remaining 24 stitches.

finishing:

Sew shoulder seams together. Sew sleeves on. Sew side and sleeve seams. With #9 needle, pick up 70 stitches around neck edge (23 stitches from each front and 24 stitches from back neck). Work in K1, P1 ribbing for 6 rows. Bind off stitches loosely. With #9 needle, pick up 68 (76, 84) stitches on left front (as worn) for button band. Work in K1, P1 ribbing for 6 rows. Bind off loosely. Pick up 68 (76, 84) stitches for right front (as worn) for buttonhole band. Work in K1, P1 ribbing for 2 rows. On row 3 make buttonholes as follows:

SMALL: Rib 3 *(YO, Rib 2tog, Rib 13) 4 times, Rib 2tog, YO, Rib 3.

MEDIUM: Rib 3 *(YO, Rib 2tog, Rib 15) 4 times, Rib 2tog, YO, Rib 3.

LARGE: Rib 3 *(YO, Rib 2tog, Rib 17) 4 times, Rib 2tog, YO, Rib 3.

Work rows 4, 5, 6 in K1, P1 ribbing. Bind off.

NOTE: On Row 3 when you are knitting over a YO (yarn over), knit the stitch through the back. If you are purling over YO (yarn over), purl as usual.

Rib 2 means K1, P1; Rib 3 means K1, P1, K1.

Buttonholes are made on 1 row only.

Buttonhole band is placed on right front (as worn) for women, and left front for men.

Repeat 4 times refers to the instructions within the parentheses().

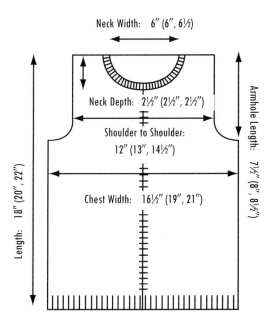

Neck Width: 6″ (6″, 6½)

Neck Depth: 2½″ (2½″, 2½″)

Shoulder to Shoulder: 12″ (13″, 14½″)

Chest Width: 16½″ (19″, 21″)

Armhole Length: 7½″ (8″, 8½″)

Length: 18″ (20″, 22″)

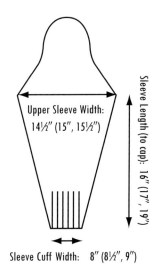

Upper Sleeve Width: 14½″ (15″, 15½″)

Sleeve Length (to cap): 16″ (17″, 19″)

Sleeve Cuff Width: 8″ (8½″, 9″)

BACK

1: KNIT ROW: Bind off 3 (4, 4) stitches, knit to end.
2: PURL ROW: Bind off 4 stitches, purl to end.

For Small & Medium, continue as follows:

3: KNIT ROW: Bind off 2 stitches, knit to end.
4: PURL ROW: Bind off 2 stitches, purl to end.
5: KNIT ROW: Bind off 2 stitches, knit to end.
6: PURL ROW: Bind off 2 stitches, purl to end.
7: KNIT ROW: Knit 1 stitch, K2tog, knit until
   3 stitches remain on left needle, K2tog, K1.
8: PURL ROW: Purl.
   Repeat rows 7 & 8 1 (3) more times.

For Large, do rows 1 & 2 and continue as follows:

3: KNIT ROW: Bind off 3 stitches, knit to end.
4: PURL ROW: Bind off 3 stitches, purl to end.
5: KNIT ROW: Bind off 2 stitches, knit to end.
6: PURL ROW: Bind off 2 stitches, purl to end.
7: KNIT ROW: Knit 1 stitch, K2tog, knit until 3
   stitches remain on left needle, K2tog, K1.
8: PURL ROW: Purl.
   Repeat rows 7 & 8 3 more times.

LEFT FRONT (left side when worn)

1: KNIT ROW: Bind off 3 (4, 4) stitches, knit to end.
2: PURL ROW: Purl.

For Small & Medium, continue as follows:

3: KNIT ROW: Bind off 2 stitches, knit to end.
4: PURL ROW: Purl.
5: KNIT ROW: Bind off 2 stitches, knit to end.
6: PURL ROW: Purl.
7: KNIT ROW: Knit 1 stitch, K2tog, knit to end of row.
8: PURL ROW: Purl.
   Repeat rows 7 & 8 1 (3) more times.

For Large, do rows 1 & 2 and continue as follows:

3: KNIT ROW: Bind off 3 stitches, knit to end.
4: PURL ROW: Purl.
5: KNIT ROW: Bind off 2 stitches, knit to end.
6: PURL ROW: Purl.
7: KNIT ROW: Knit 1 stitch, K2tog, knit to end of row.
8: PURL ROW: Purl.
   Repeat rows 7 & 8 3 more times.

RIGHT FRONT (right side when worn)

1: PURL ROW: Bind off 3 (4, 4) stitches, purl to
   end.
2: KNIT ROW: Knit.

For Small & Medium, continue as follows:

3: PURL ROW: Bind off 2 stitches, purl to end.
4: KNIT ROW: Knit.
5: PURL ROW: Bind off 2 stitches, purl to end.
6: KNIT ROW: Knit to last 3 stitches, K2tog, K1.
7: PURL ROW: Purl.
   Repeat rows 6 & 7 1 (3) more times.

For Large, do rows 1 & 2 and continue as follows:

3: PURL ROW: Bind off 3 stitches, purl to end.
4: KNIT ROW: Knit.
5: PURL ROW: Bind off 2 stitches, purl to end.
6: KNIT ROW: Knit to last 3 stitches, K2tog, K1.
7: PURL ROW: Purl.
   Repeat rows 6 & 7 3 more times.

LEFT FRONT (left side when worn)

1: PURL ROW: Bind off 4 stitches, purl to end.
2: KNIT ROW: Knit.
3: PURL ROW: Bind off 3 stitches, purl to end.
4: KNIT ROW: Knit.
5: PURL ROW: Bind off 2 stitches, purl to end.
6: KNIT ROW: Knit.
7: PURL ROW: Bind off 1 stitch, purl to end.
   Repeat rows 6 & 7 2 (2, 3) more times.

RIGHT FRONT (right side when worn)

1: KNIT ROW: Bind off 4 stitches, knit to end.
2: PURL ROW: Purl.
3: KNIT ROW: Bind off 3 stitches, knit to end.
4: PURL ROW: Purl.
5: KNIT ROW: Bind off 2 stitches, knit to end.
6: PURL ROW: Purl.
7: KNIT ROW: Bind off 1 stitch, knit to end.
   Repeat rows 6 & 7 2 (2, 3) more times.

• When you are done with the bind-off instructions,
  measure the length of the front piece, comparing it
  to the length of the back. If the front and back
  measure the same, bind off the remaining stitches.

V-Neck Pullovers

It should go without saying that the only difference between your basic V-neck and your basic crewneck is how you shape the neck. However, even this slight variation can make two sweaters look completely different from one another. A V-neck can also be a bit more elegant—or a little sexier—than its preppy crewneck cousin. We think V-necks flatter just about everyone. Here is your chance to practice common decreases such as K2tog and SSK in order to shape your neck.

Stripes Are Stars is the simplest sweater in this group. There is no ribbing anywhere, just knitting and purling the whole way. We chose fluffy yarn and as a result the bottoms did not roll and the yarn hid the ragged neck edges that can sometimes occur when shaping a neck (this is why we usually put an edging on the neck). Depending on the yarn you choose, your bottom and your cuffs might roll and your neck might need some finishing work. Not Your Standard-Issue Sweatshirt is a unique sweater. It has a high V-neck and we put a seed-stitch edging on it while we were knitting. We also added a hood, which you don't need to include if it's not your thing; the sweater looks great with or without. Also remember that you can always make your V higher by starting the shaping later, or lower by starting it lower. Bare That Belly is a standard V-neck sweater with ribs at the bottom, cuffs, and neck. The finishing at the neck is the most challenging aspect, but it is still very doable.

stripes are stars

You know how some people have a trademark look that only they can carry off? Well, let us tell you about Linda. She does not wear solid colors. Plaid pants paired with a striped shirt are par for the course with her. How is this relevant? When Linda, a beginner knitter, wanted to make her first sweater, she was dead set on stripes. Striping is not hard, but it can be a little intimidating for a beginner. Fortunately for Linda, we had a variegated yarn that makes stripes by itself. All you do is knit and purl and voilà, stripes appear. If only everything could be so easy and look so fabulous. And even without the stripes it's a wonderful shape you'll want in lots of colors.

YARN: Noro Implessions (55 yards/40g ball)
COLOR: #5
AMOUNT: 8 (9, 10) balls
TOTAL YARDAGE: 440 yards (495 yards, 550 yards)
GAUGE: 2 stitches = 1"; 8 stitches = 4 inches
NEEDLE SIZE: US 15 (10mm) or size needed to obtain gauge
SIZES: S (M, L)

back:

With #15 needle, cast on 40 (42, 46) stitches. Work in St st until piece measures 15" (16½", 17") from cast-on edge, ending with a WS row. **SHAPE ARMHOLES:** Bind off 3 stitches at the beginning of the next 2 rows. Bind off 2 stitches at the beginning of the next 2 rows. Then decrease 1 stitch at each edge every other row 1 (1, 2) times until 28 (30, 32) stitches remain. Continue in St st until piece measures 23½" (25", 26") from cast-on edge. Bind off remaining stitches.

front:

Work as for back until piece measures 15" (16½", 17"). **SHAPE ARMHOLES AS FOR BACK.** Continue in St st until piece measures 17½" (19", 19½") from cast-on edge, ending on a WS row. NOTE: You may still be shaping the armhole as you are shaping the neck.

SHAPE V NECK: Place a marker around needle in center of work (see page 50), then shape V as follows: Row 1: Knit to 4 stitches before the marker, K2tog, K2. Turn work. Row 2: Purl to end of row. Repeat rows 1 & 2 6 (7, 7) more times until 7 (7, 8) stitches remain. Continue in St st until piece measures same as back. Bind off

remaining stitches. Attach yarn to remaining stitches and shape V as follows: Row 1: K2, SSK, knit to end of row. Turn work. Row 2: Purl. Repeat rows 1 & 2 6 (7, 7) times until 7 (7, 8) stitches remain. Work until piece measures same as back. Bind off remaining stitches. NOTE: K2tog = knit 2 stitches together. SSK, slip, slip, knit = slip 2 stitches onto right needle as if to knit them, insert left needle into front of stitches, and knit the 2 stitches together.

sleeves:

With #15 needle, cast on 20 (20, 22) stitches. Work in St st. At the same time, increase 1 stitch at each edge every 8th row 6 (6, 6) times until you have 32 (32, 34) stitches. Continue in St st until sleeve measures 20" (20½", 21"). NOTE: Increase leaving 2 edge stitches on either side of work. This means you should knit 2 stitches, increase a stitch, knit to the last 2 stitches, increase a stitch, and then knit the remaining 2 stitches. Increasing like this makes it easier to sew up your seams. **SHAPE CAP:** Bind off 3 stitches at the beginning of the next 2 rows. Bind off 2 stitches at the beginning of the next 2 rows. Then decrease 1 stitch at each end every other row 1 time. Bind off

2 stitches at the beginning of the next 6 rows. Bind off the remaining 8 (8, 10) stitches.

finishing:

Sew shoulder seams together. Sew on sleeves. Sew side and sleeve seams.

1: KNIT ROW: Bind off 3 stitches, knit to end.
2: PURL ROW: Bind off 3 stitches, purl to end.
3: KNIT ROW: Bind off 2 stitches, knit to end.
4: PURL ROW: Bind off 2 stitches, purl to end.
5: KNIT ROW: Knit 1 stitch, K2tog, knit until 3 stitches remain on left needle, K2tog, K1.
6: PURL ROW: Purl.
   Repeat rows 5 & 6 0 (0, 1) more times.

First you must place a marker around the needle in the center of the work.

1: KNIT ROW: Knit to 4 stitches before the marker, K2tog, K2. Turn work.
2: PURL ROW: Purl.
   Repeat rows 1 & 2 6 (7, 7) more times.

Attach yarn to the other side of the V.

1: KNIT ROW: K2, SSK, knit to end of row.
2: PURL ROW: Purl.
   Repeat rows 1 & 2 6 (7, 7) more times.

• When you are done with the bind-off instructions, measure the length of the front piece, comparing it to the length of the back. If the front and back measure the same, bind off the remaining stitches. If the front is too short, continue knitting and purling until the pieces are of equal length, then bind off.

• If you are using a self-striping yarn, when you start shaping your V-neck you may want to wind through a second ball of yarn to find the same color point before attaching it to start the second side.

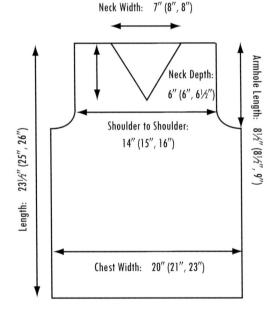

Neck Width: 7" (8", 8")

Neck Depth: 6" (6", 6½")

Armhole Length: 8½" (8½", 9")

Shoulder to Shoulder: 14" (15", 16")

Length: 23½" (25", 26")

Chest Width: 20" (21", 23")

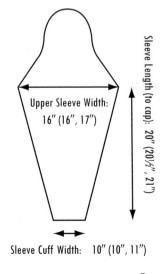

Upper Sleeve Width: 16" (16", 17")

Sleeve Length (to cap): 20" (20½", 21")

Sleeve Cuff Width: 10" (10", 11")

not your standard-issue sweatshirt

Sometimes all a girl needs is her knitting project, a fuzzy pair of socks, and her favorite faded, ratty sweatshirt. Sometimes, however, you're in a sweatshirt mood but that beat-up, smelly thing you've been wearing to the gym every day just isn't appropriate. For those times, this sweater is just the ticket. It's got the comfortable feeling of a sweatshirt but with a little more flair, a little more style. You can still wear it to curl up on the couch or to go to the gym, but you can also wear it out to dinner or on a date. You may find you live in it!

YARN: Manos Del Uruguay (135 yards/100g ball)
COLOR: 49
AMOUNT: 7 (8, 8) balls
TOTAL YARDAGE: 945 yards (1,080 yards, 1,080 yards)
GAUGE: 4 stitches = 1 inch; 16 stitches = 4 inches
NEEDLE SIZE: US 9 (5½mm) or size needed to obtain gauge
SIZES: S (M, L)

back:

With #9 needle, cast on 78 (82, 88) stitches. Work in seed-stitch border: Row 1: K1, P1 across row. Row 2: P1, K1 across row. Work rows 1 & 2 for 6 rows. Then work in St st, keeping the first and last 6 stitches in seed stitch, for 4". Row 1: *(K1, P1)* 3 times. Knit to the last 6 stitches, *(K1, P1)* 3 times. Row 2: *(P1, K1)* 3 times, purl to the last 6 stitches, *(P1, K1)* 3 times. Continue in all St st until piece measures 12" (13½", 15") from cast-on edge. **SHAPE ARMHOLES:** Bind off 4 stitches at the beginning of the next 2 rows. Bind off 3 stitches at the beginning of the next 2 rows, then bind off 2 stitches at the beginning of the next 2 rows. Then decrease 1 stitch each edge every other row 0 (1, 3) times until 60 (62, 64) stitches remain. Continue in St st until piece measures 20" (22", 24") from cast-on edge. Bind off remaining stitches.

front:

Work as for back until piece measures 12" (13½", 15"). **SHAPE ARMHOLES AS FOR BACK.** Continue in St st until piece measures 15" (17", 18") from cast-on edge, ending on a WS row. **SHAPE V-NECK:** Place a marker around needle in center of work (see page 50), then shape V as follows: Row 1: Knit to 8 stitches before the marker, K2tog, work the last 6 stitches *(K1, P1)* 3 times. Turn work. Row 2: *(P1, K1)* 3 times. Purl to end of row. Repeat rows 1 & 2 14 (14, 15) more times until 15 (16, 16) stitches remain. When piece measures same as back, bind off remaining stitches. Attach yarn to remaining stitches and shape V as follows: Row 1: *(K1, P1)* 3 times, SSK, knit to end of row. Row 2: Purl to last 6 stitches *(P1, K1)* 3 times. Repeat rows 1 & 2 14 (14, 15) more times until 15 (16, 16) stitches remain. Work until piece measures same as back. Bind off remaining stitches. NOTE: K2tog = knit 2 stitches together. SSK, slip, slip, knit = slip 2 stitches onto right needle as if to knit them, insert left needle into front of stitches, and knit the 2 stitches together.

sleeves:

With #9 needle, cast on 34 (34, 36) stitches. Work in seed stitch: Row 1: K1, P1 across row. Row 2: P1, K1 across row. Work rows 1 & 2 for 6 rows. Continue in St st. At the same time, increase 1 stitch at each edge every 6th row 13 (14, 16) times until you have 60 (62, 68) stitches. Continue in St st until sleeve measures 16" (17", 18"). NOTE: Increase leaving 2 edge stitches on either side of work. This means you should knit 2 stitches, increase a stitch, knit to the last 2 stitches, increase a stitch, and then knit the remaining 2 stitches. Increasing like this makes it easier to sew up your seams.

SHAPE CAP: Bind off 4 stitches at the beginning of the next 2 rows. Bind off 3 stitches at the beginning of the next 2 rows. Bind off 2 stitches at the beginning of the next 2 rows. Then decrease 1 stitch at each end every other row 12 times. Bind off remaining 18 (20, 26) stitches.

hood:

With #9 needle, cast on 42 stitches. Work in St st, keeping the first 10 stitches in seed stitch: Row 1: *(K1, P1)* 5 times, knit to end. Row 2: Purl to last 10 stitches *(P1, K1)* 5 times. When piece measures 26″, bind off.

finishing:

Sew shoulder seams together. Sew sleeves on. Sew hood on. Sew sleeve and side seams.

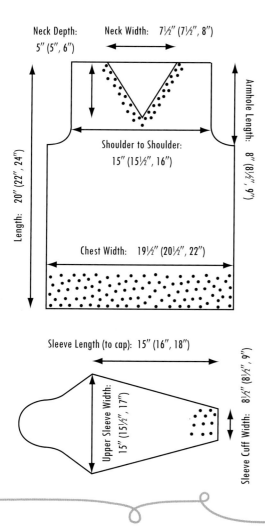

Neck Depth: 5″ (5″, 6″)

Neck Width: 7½″ (7½″, 8″)

Armhole Length: 8″ (8½″, 9″)

Shoulder to Shoulder: 15″ (15½″, 16″)

Length: 20″ (22″, 24″)

Chest Width: 19½″ (20½″, 22″)

Sleeve Length (to cap): 15″ (16″, 18″)

Upper Sleeve Width: 15″ (15½″, 17″)

Sleeve Cuff Width: 8½″ (8½″, 9″)

bare that belly

Lisa just got her belly button pierced and wanted to knit herself a cropped sweater that would show off that little hoop as well as her washboard abs. She made this sexy little number, which she wears with a great pair of faded, low-slung jeans. Of course, if you're of a more modest persuasion, you can make the same sweater longer by knitting an extra few inches before you begin the armhole shaping. The choice is yours.

YARN: Filatura Di Crosa Zara (136½ yards/50g ball)
COLOR: #1656
AMOUNT: 11 (12, 14) balls
TOTAL YARDAGE: 1,504 yards (1,640 yards, 1,914 yards)
GAUGE: 3½ stitches = 1"; 14 stitches = 4 inches
NEEDLE SIZE: US 10½ (7mm) for the body & US 9 (5½mm) for the ribbing or sizes needed to obtain gauge
SIZES: S (M, L)

Yarn is worked doubled throughout the sweater—this means you should hold 2 strands of yarn together as though they are 1.

back:

With #9 needle and 2 strands of yarn, cast on 60 (63, 72) stitches. For Small & Large: Work in K3, P3 ribbing for 4 rows. For Medium: Row 1: K3 *(P3, K3)* to end. Row 2: P3 *(K3, P3)* to end. Repeat rows 1 & 2 twice. **FOR MEDIUM ONLY:** Increase 1 stitch on last row of ribbing (64 stitches total). For all sizes, switch to 10½ needles and work in St st until piece measures 11" (12", 13") from cast-on edge, ending with a WS row. **SHAPE ARMHOLES:** Bind off 3 stitches at the beginning of the next 2 rows. Bind off 2 stitches at the beginning of the next 2 rows. Then decrease 1 stitch at each edge every other row 1 (2, 5) times until 48 (50, 52) stitches remain. Continue in St st until piece measures 18½" (20", 22") from cast-on edge. Bind off remaining stitches.

front:

Work as for back until piece measures 11" (12", 13"). **SHAPE ARMHOLES AS FOR BACK.** Continue in St st until piece measures 13½" (14", 16") from cast-on edge, ending on a WS row. **SHAPE V-NECK:** Place a marker around needle in center of work (see page 50), then shape V as follows: Row 1: Knit to 4 stitches before the marker, K2 tog, K2. Turn work. Row 2: Purl to end of row. Repeat rows 1 & 2 9 more times until 14 (15, 16) stitches remain. Continue in St st until piece measures same as back. Bind off remaining stitches. Attach yarn to remaining stitches and shape V as follows: Row 1: K2, SSK, knit to end of row. Turn work. Row 2: Purl. Repeat rows 1 & 2 9 more times until 14 (15, 16) stitches remain. Continue in St st until piece measures same as back. Bind off remaining stitches. NOTE: K2tog = knit 2 stitches together. SSK, slip, slip, knit = slip 2 stitches onto right needle as if to knit them, insert left needle into front of stitches, and knit the 2 stitches together.

sleeves:

With #9 needle and 2 strands of yarn, cast on 30 (30, 33) stitches. Work in K3, P3 ribbing as follows: For Small & Medium: K3, P3 ribbing for 4 rows. For Large: Row 1: K3 *(P3, K3)* to end. Row 2: P3 *(K3, P3)* to end. Repeat rows 1 & 2 2 times for a total of 4 rows. Change to #10½ needle and continue in St st. At the same time, increase 1 stitch at each edge every 6th row 9 (8, 8) times until you have 48 (46, 49) stitches and then every 4th row 2 (4, 5) times until you have 52 (54, 59) stitches. Continue in St st until sleeve measures 15½″ (16½″, 17½″). **NOTE:** Increase leaving 2 edge stitches on either side of work. This means you should knit 2 stitches, increase a stitch, knit to the last 2 stitches, increase a stitch, and then knit the remaining 2 stitches. Increasing like this makes it easier to sew up your seams. **SHAPE CAP:** Bind off 3 stitches at the beginning of the next 2 rows. Bind off 2 stitches at the beginning of the next 2 rows. Then decrease 1 stitch at each end every other row 1 (2, 5) times. Bind off 2 stitches at the beginning of the next 12 (12, 10) rows. Bind off the remaining 16 (16, 19) stitches.

finishing:

Sew shoulders together. Attach sleeves to body of sweater and sew sleeve and side seams together. For V-neck finishing: With a 16-inch #9 circular needle, starting at left neck edge, pick up 20 stitches down left side of neck, place marker, pick up 2 stitches in middle of neck, place marker, pick up 20 stitches up right neck edge, and pick up 24 stitches on back of neck. Place a marker to mark the beginning and end of the round. Join yarn. Working in a circle, work in K2, P2 ribbing, making sure that 2 knit stitches are between the markers. Work as follows: K2, P2 until 2 stitches before center marker, SSK, slip marker, K2, slip marker, K2tog, K2, P2 until end of round. Repeat this 3 more times. Bind off loosely.

STEP-BY-STEP GUIDE TO SHAPING THE ARMHOLE

1: KNIT ROW: Bind off 3 stitches, knit to end.
2: PURL ROW: Bind off 3 stitches, purl to end.
3: KNIT ROW: Bind off 2 stitches, knit to end.
4: PURL ROW: Bind off 2 stitches, purl to end.
5: KNIT ROW: Knit 1 stitch, K2tog, knit until 3 stitches remain on left needle, K2tog, K1.
6: PURL ROW: Purl.
   Repeat rows 5 & 6 0 (1, 4) more times.

STEP-BY-STEP GUIDE TO SHAPING THE V-NECK

First you must place a marker around the needle in the center of the work.

1: KNIT ROW: Knit to 4 stitches before the marker, K2tog, K2.
2: PURL ROW: Purl.
   Repeat rows 1 & 2 9 (9, 9) more times.

Attach yarn to the other side of the V.

1: KNIT ROW: K2, SSK, knit to end of row.
2: PURL ROW: Purl.
   Repeat rows 1 & 2 9 (9, 9) more times.

• When you are done with the bind-off instructions, measure the length of the front piece, comparing it to the length of the back. If the back and front measure the same, bind off the remaining stitches. If the front is too short, continue knitting and purling until the pieces are of equal length, then bind off.

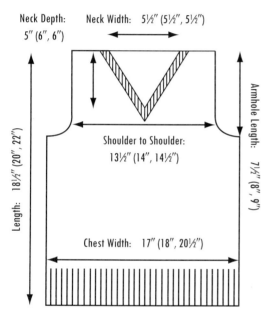

Neck Depth: 5" (6", 6")

Neck Width: 5½" (5½", 5½")

Shoulder to Shoulder: 13½" (14", 14½")

Armhole Length: 7½" (8", 9")

Length: 18½" (20", 22")

Chest Width: 17" (18", 20½")

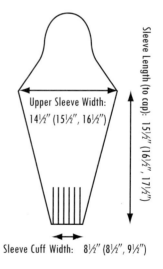

Upper Sleeve Width: 14½" (15½", 16½")

Sleeve Length (to cap): 15½" (16½", 17½")

Sleeve Cuff Width: 8½" (8½", 9½")

Tank Tops

Tank tops are quick projects that are great for someone who wants to ease back into knitting. These nifty tops do require neck and armhole shaping, but you can put sleeves and increasing on hold until you've built up your confidence. Even if you're a seasoned pro, though, you'll love knitting these tanks to wear under a suit, with shorts, or for a summer party. Because the investment in time is so modest, we know you'll be back for more.

We have three different tank shapes in this chapter. *Oooh Baby* is knit in a winter yarn, but the shape can be made as a summer tank too. Basically this is just a basic crewneck pullover without sleeves and with a turtleneck. *Sexy Summer Tank* is the standard tank top shape with neck shaping on the front and the back and two small straps at the top. *Summer in the City* is a funkier shape that combines steep armhole decrease with crocheted straps.

oooh baby

It may be winter, but that doesn't mean you can't show off your sexy shoulders. Let's face it, sleeveless turtlenecks are incredibly flattering and can be dressed up or down easily. And no sleeves—what could be better, right? Knit it up Friday night to wear out Saturday night. And remember, even if this trend goes out of vogue, you can always buy some extra yarn and add sleeves.

YARN: Tahki Baby (60 yards/ 100g ball)
COLOR: A: 9, B: 10
AMOUNT: 4 (4, 5) balls color A; 1 ball color B
TOTAL YARDAGE: 240 yards (240 yards, 300 yards)
GAUGE: 2 stitches = 1 inch; 8 stitches = 4 inches
NEEDLE SIZE: US 15 (10mm) or size needed to obtain gauge
SIZES: S (M, L)

This pattern requires an edge stitch—this means you must always knit the first and last stitch.

back:

With #15 needle and color A, cast on 32 (35, 41) stitches. Work in K3, P3 ribbing as follows: For Small: Rows 1 & 2: K1 edge stitch, *K3, P3* to end, K1 edge stitch. Work rows 1 & 2 until piece measures 5″. For Medium & Large: Row 1: K1 edge stitch, K3, *(P3, K3)* to end, K1 edge stitch. Row 2: K1 edge stitch, P3, *(K3, P3)* to end, K1 edge stitch. Then work in St st until piece measures 12″ (12½″, 14″) from cast-on edge, ending with a WS row. **SHAPE ARMHOLES:** Bind off 2 stitches at the beginning of the next 2 rows. Then decrease 1 stitch at each edge every other row 2 (2, 3) times, until 24 (27, 31) stitches remain. Continue to work in St st until piece measures 18″ (20″, 22″) from cast-on edge. Bind off remaining stitches.

front:

Work as for back until piece measures 12″ (12½″, 14″). **SHAPE ARMHOLES AS FOR BACK.**

Continue in St st until piece measures 15½″ (17½″, 19½″) from cast-on edge, ending with a WS row. **SHAPE NECK:** Bind off center 6 (7, 7) stitches. Working each side of neck separately, at the beginning of each neck edge every other row bind off 2 stitches 1 time, 1 stitch 2 (2, 3) times. Continue working in St st on remaining 5 (6, 7) stitches until piece measures same as back. Bind off remaining stitches.

finishing:

Sew shoulder seams together. Sew side seams. With a #13 16-inch circular needle, pick up 30 (36, 36) stitches around neck and work in K3, P3 ribbing for 7½″. Work 1 row of purl. Change to color B and bind off very loosely with color B. Work 1 row of single crochet around armholes in color A.

1: KNIT ROW: Bind off 2 stitches, knit to end.
2: PURL ROW: Bind off 2 stitches, purl to end.
3: KNIT ROW: Knit 1 stitch, K2tog, knit until 3 stitches remain on left needle, K2tog, K1.
4: PURL ROW: Purl.
   Repeat rows 3 & 4 1 (0, 2) more times.

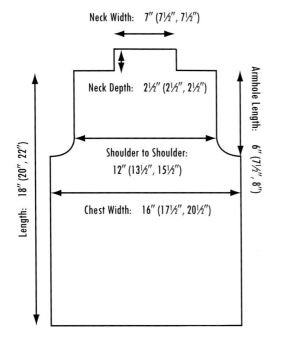

Neck Width: 7" (7½", 7½")

Neck Depth: 2½" (2½", 2½")

Armhole Length: 6" (7½", 8")

Shoulder to Shoulder: 12" (13½", 15½")

Chest Width: 16" (17½", 20½")

Length: 18" (20", 22")

1: KNIT ROW: Knit 11 (13, 14) stitches; with the 10th (12th, 13th) stitch, begin to bind off the center 6 (7, 7) stitches. For example, for size Small, this means you should pull the 10th stitch over the 11th stitch. After binding off the center stitches, check to make sure you have 9 (11, 12) stitches on each side of the hole including the stitch on the right needle. Knit to end of row. Turn work.
2: PURL ROW: Purl 1 row. Turn work.
3: KNIT ROW: Bind off first 2 stitches. Knit to end of row. Turn work.
4: PURL ROW: Purl 1 row. Turn work.
5: KNIT ROW: Bind off 1 stitch. Knit to end of row. Turn work.
6: PURL ROW: Purl 1 row. Turn work.
   Repeat rows 5 & 6 1 (2, 2) more times.

• When you are done with the bind-off instructions, measure the length of the front piece, comparing it to the length of the back. If the front and the back measure the same, bind off the remaining stitches. If the front is too short, continue knitting and purling until the pieces are of equal length, then bind off.

• Attach the yarn to the other side of the neck edge and begin binding off 2 stitches immediately. You will now be binding off when you are purling. Finish the neck shaping as for the other side and bind off.

sexy summer tank

When late winter rolls around, what are you dreaming of? Is it summer? That's what we're waiting for. No more heavy coats, gloves, mittens, galoshes. Just nice, light clothing. If the temperature outside is frigid, think about knitting a sexy tank top that you can wear once the ice thaws. This one is fast and easy to knit, and nothing will keep you cooler in the summer heat.

YARN: Prism, Diana (60 yards/50g ball)
COLOR: Jellybean
AMOUNT: 4 (5, 6) balls
TOTAL YARDAGE: 240 yards (300 yards, 360 yards)
GAUGE: 2¾ stitches = 1 inch; 11 stitches = 4 inches.
NEEDLE SIZE: US 13 (9mm) or size needed to obtain gauge
SIZES: S (M, L)

back & front (make 2)

With #13 needle, cast on 40 (44, 50) stitches. Work in St st until piece measures 10½″ (11½″, 13″) from cast-on edge, ending with a WS row. **SHAPE ARMHOLES:** Bind off 3 stitches at the beginning of the next 2 rows. Bind off 2 stitches at the beginning of the next 2 rows. Then decrease 1 stitch at each edge every other row 3 (4, 6) times, until 24 (26, 28) stitches remain. Continue to work in St st until piece measures 14″ (16″, 18″) from cast-on edge. **SHAPE CREW-NECK:** Bind off the center 6 (8, 8) stitches. Working each side of neck separately, at the beginning of each neck edge every other row bind off 2 stitches 1 time, 1 stitch 3 (3, 4) times. Continue working in St st on remaining 4 (4, 4) stitches until piece measures 17″ (19″, 21″) from cast-on edge. Bind off remaining stitches.

finishing:

Sew shoulder seams together. Sew side seams. With a size J crochet hook, work 1 row of single crochet around neck edge and armhole edges.

STEP-BY-STEP GUIDE TO SHAPING THE ARMHOLE

1: KNIT ROW: Bind off 3 stitches, knit to end.
2: PURL ROW: Bind off 3 stitches, purl to end.
3: KNIT ROW: Bind off 2 stitches, knit to end.
4: PURL ROW: Bind off 2 stitches, purl to end.
5: KNIT ROW: Knit 1 stitch, K2tog, knit until 3 stitches remain on left needle, K2tog, K1.
6: PURL ROW: Purl.
   Repeat rows 5 & 6 2 (3, 5) more times.

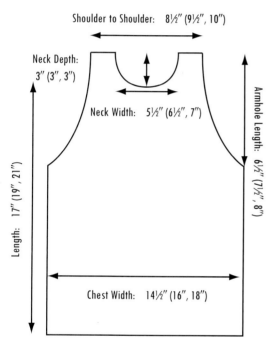

Shoulder to Shoulder: 8½" (9½", 10")

Neck Depth: 3" (3", 3")

Neck Width: 5½" (6½", 7")

Armhole Length: 6½" (7½", 8")

Length: 17" (19", 21")

Chest Width: 14½" (16", 18")

STEP-BY-STEP GUIDE TO SHAPING THE CREWNECK

1: KNIT ROW: Knit 11(11, 12) stitches; with the 10th (10th, 11th) stitch begin to bind off the center 6 (8, 8) stitches. For example, for Small, this means you should pull the 10th stitch over the 11th stitch. After binding off the center stitches, check to make sure you have 9 (9, 10) stitches on each side of the hole including the stitch on the right needle. Knit to end of row. Turn work.

Note: Remember that after binding off the center stitches, you will work one side of the neck at a time.

2: PURL ROW: Purl 1 row. Turn work.
3: KNIT ROW: Bind off first 2 stitches. Knit to end of row. Turn work.
4: PURL ROW: Purl 1 row. Turn work.
5: KNIT ROW: Bind off 1 stitch. Knit to end of row. Turn work.
6: PURL ROW: Purl 1 row. Turn work.
   Repeat rows 5 & 6 2 (2, 3) more times.

• When you are done with the bind-off instructions, measure the length of the front piece, comparing it to the length of the back. If the front and back measure the same, bind off the remaining stitches. If the front is too short, continue knitting and purling until the pieces are of equal length, then bind off.

• Attach yarn to the other side of the neck edge and begin binding off 2 stitches immediately. You will now be binding off when you are purling. Finish neck shaping as for the other side and bind off.

summer in the city

Jordana's friend Julien was in a knitting funk. She still had a sleeve to go on the sweater she was making for her six-foot-six brother-in-law with the twenty-three-inch arms, and she was stuck somewhere in the middle of a sweater she was knitting for herself on size 4 needles that was going very slowly. What Julien needed was some instant gratification. She came into the store, saw this tank, and knew it was just what the doctor ordered. She made the tank top over the weekend and wore it to work under her suit on Monday.

YARN: GGH Mystik (115 yards/50g ball) & S. Charles Mystique
(104 yards/50g ball)
COLOR: Mystik #60; Mystique #50
AMOUNT: 3 (4, 4) balls of each yarn
TOTAL YARDAGE: Mystik: 345 yards (460 yards, 460 yards);
Mystique 312 yards (416 yards, 416 yards)
GAUGE: 4 stitches = 1"; 6 rows = 1"; 16 stiches = 4 inches; 24 rows
= 4 inches
NEEDLE SIZE: US 9 (5½mm) or size needed to obtain gauge.
SIZES: S (M, L)

Yarn is worked doubled throughout sweater—this means you should hold 1 strand of Mystik and 1 strand of Mystique together and work them as though they are 1.

back:

With #9 needle and 1 strand of each yarn, cast on 58 (64, 72) stitches. Work in St st until piece measures 12½" (13", 14½"). **SHAPE ARMHOLES:** Bind off 3 (4, 5) stitches at beginning of next 2 rows. Then decrease 1 stitch each edge alternating every 4th and every 2nd row 6 times until 40 (44, 50) stitches remain. Then decrease 1 stitch each end every 2nd row 6 (7, 8) times until 28 (30, 34) stitches remain. Purl 1 row. Bind off remaining stitches.

front:

Work as for back until piece measures 12½" (13", 14½"). **SHAPE ARMHOLES:** Bind off 3 (4, 5) stitches at beginning of next 2 rows. Then decrease 1 stitch each edge every other row 12 (13, 14) times until 28 (30 34) stitches remain. Purl 1 row. Bind off remaining stitches.

finishing:

Sew side seams together. With an I (5.5mm) crochet hook, work 1 row single crochet around armholes, making a chain to connect the two neck edges (16–18 chains or to desired length). Single-crochet around neck and bottom edges.

MAKING A
CHAIN STITCH
With the crochet hook, just pull yarn through the existing loop on the crochet hook and you have made a chain stitch.

BACK:

1: KNIT ROW: Bind off 3 (4, 5) stitches, knit to end.
2: PURL ROW: Bind off 3 (4, 5) stitches, purl to end.
3: KNIT ROW: Knit 1 stitch, K2tog, knit until 3 stitches remain on left needle, K2tog, K1.
4: PURL ROW: Purl.
5: KNIT ROW: Knit.
6: PURL ROW: Purl.
7: KNIT ROW: Knit 1 stitch, K2tog, knit until 3 stitches remain on left needle, K2tog, K1.
8: PURL ROW: Purl.
   Repeat rows 3–8 2 more times.
   Then repeat rows 7 & 8 6 (7, 8) more times.

FRONT:

1: KNIT ROW: Bind off 3 (4, 5) stitches, knit to end.
2: PURL ROW: Bind off 3 (4, 5) stitches, purl to end.
3: KNIT ROW: Knit 1 stitch, K2tog, knit until 3 stitches remain on left needle, K2tog, K1.
4: PURL ROW: Purl.
   Repeat rows 3 & 4 11 (12, 13) more times.

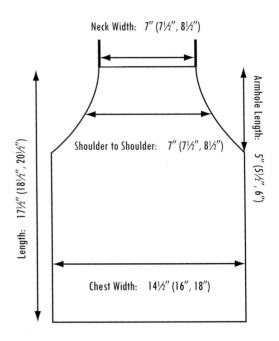

Neck Width: 7″ (7½″, 8½″)

Armhole Length: 5″ (5½″, 6″)

Shoulder to Shoulder: 7″ (7½″, 8½″)

Length: 17½″ (18½″, 20½″)

Chest Width: 14½″ (16″, 18″)

Men's Sweaters

Okay, call us unromantic, but we *never* advocate making a sweater as the way to a man's heart. Better to develop a passion for baseball statistics or cultivate your knowledge of esoteric audio components. If it's the real deal, though, and you want to make the ultimate romantic gesture (or simply need to institute a wardrobe upgrade), nothing beats a sweater you've knit your guy yourself.

Surprisingly, men's sweater patterns are not so easy to find. And even more curious, simple ones are virtually nonexistent. We've come up with three great sweater shapes for men that he'll wear without a fight. We chose a roll neck, a turtleneck, and a standard V-neck. *He'll Wear It Every Day* is a very easy sweater that is knit entirely in stockinette stitch. It's a nice, casual look that is a little oversized and extremely comfortable. And it's true that if you make this sweater for him he'll want to wear it every day. *The Compromise* turtleneck is just your average crewneck knit longer. It's a great, warm, soft, snuggly sweater that looks terrific with jeans or can be dressed up and worn with a nice pair of pants. (If the guy you're knitting for feels too confined in a turtleneck but likes this style, just knit a 1-inch ribbing instead of a 7-inch one and he'll have a crewneck instead of a turtleneck.) *The Exception to the Rule* uses a yarn that we love but we felt was unbearably thin to knit such a large garment. So we doubled the yarn and made a standard V-neck with ribs at all edges.

he'll wear it every day

Carrie wanted to make a sweater for her husband, David, but he had bad childhood memories of having to wear the sweaters his grandmother knit him: One sleeve was always longer than the other or there would be a strange hole smack-dab in the front. Despite David's protests, Carrie went ahead and knit him this sweater. It turned out so well he almost never goes out the door without it. In fact, David wants to know when she's going to make him another one—this time in navy blue cashmere.

YARN: Rowan Chunky Tweed (109 yards/100g ball)
COLOR: 953 (Herb)
AMOUNT: 8 (9, 9) balls
TOTAL YARDAGE: 872 yards (981 yards, 981 yards)
GAUGE: 3¼ stitches = 1 inch; 13 stitches = 4 inches
NEEDLE SIZE: US 10½ (7mm) or size needed to obtain gauge
SIZES: S (M, L)

back:

With #10½ needle, cast on 78 (82, 84) stitches. Work in St st until piece measures 16″ (17″, 18″) from cast-on edge, ending with a WS row. **SHAPE ARMHOLES:** Bind off 4 stitches at the beginning of the next 2 rows. Bind off 3 stitches at the beginning of the next 2 rows. Bind off 2 stitches at the beginning of the following 2 rows. Then decrease 1 stitch at each edge every other row 1 time, until 58 (62, 64) stitches remain. Continue to work in St st until piece measures 25″ (27″, 28″) from cast-on edge. Bind off remaining stitches.

front:

Work as for back until piece measures 16″ (17″, 18″). **SHAPE ARMHOLES AS FOR BACK.** Continue in St st until piece measures 22½″ (24½″, 25½″) from cast-on edge, ending with a WS row. **SHAPE CREWNECK:** Bind off center 10 stitches. Working each side of neck separately, at the beginning of each neck edge every other row bind off 3 stitches 1 time, 2 stitches 2 times, 1 stitch 3 (4, 4) times. Continue working in St st on remaining 14 (15, 16) stitches until piece measures 25″ (27″, 28″) from cast-on edge. Bind off remaining stitches.

sleeves:

With #10½ needle, cast on 32 (32, 34) stitches. Work in St st. At the same time, increase 1 stitch at each edge every 6th row 12 (12, 14) times until you have 56 (56, 62) stitches. Continue in St st until sleeve measures 20″ (21″, 22″). **NOTE:** Increase leaving 2 edge stitches on either side of work. This means you should knit 2 stitches, increase a stitch, knit to the last 2 stitches, increase a stitch, and then knit the remaining 2 stitches. Increasing like this makes it easier to sew up your seams. **SHAPE CAP:** Bind off 4 stitches at the beginning of the next 2 rows. Bind off 3 stitches at the beginning of the next 2 rows. Bind off 2 stitches at the beginning of the next 2 rows. Then bind off 1 stitch at the beginning of the next 2 rows. Bind off remaining 36 (36, 42) stitches.

finishing:

Sew shoulder seams together. Sew sleeves on. Sew side and sleeve seams. With a #10½ 16-inch circular needle, pick up 68 stitches around neck and work in St st (all knit when working in the round) for 12 rows. Bind off loosely.

1: KNIT ROW: Bind off 4 stitches, knit to end.
2: PURL ROW: Bind off 4 stitches, purl to end.
3: KNIT ROW: Bind off 3 stitches, knit to end.
4: PURL ROW: Bind off 3 stitches, purl to end.
5: KNIT ROW: Bind off 2 stitches, knit to end.
6: PURL ROW: Bind off 2 stitches, purl to end.
7: KNIT ROW: Knit 1 stitch, K2tog, knit until 3 stitches remain on left needle, K2tog, K1.
8: PURL ROW: Purl.

1: KNIT ROW: Knit 26 (28, 29) stitches; with the 25th (27th, 28th) stitch begin to bind off the center 10 stitches. For example, for size Small, this means you should pull the 25th stitch over the 26th stitch. When you are done binding off the center stitches, check to make sure you have 24 (26, 27) stitches on each side of the hole including the stitch on the right needle. Knit to end of row. Turn work.
Remember that after binding off the center stitches, you will work one side of the neck at a time.
2: PURL ROW: Purl 1 row. Turn work.
3: KNIT ROW: Bind off first 3 stitches. Knit to end of row. Turn work.
4: PURL ROW: Purl 1 row. Turn work.
5: KNIT ROW: Bind off first 2 stitches. Knit to end of row. Turn work.
6: PURL ROW: Purl 1 row. Turn work.
7: KNIT ROW: Bind off first 2 stitches. Knit to end of row. Turn work.
8: PURL ROW: Purl 1 row. Turn work.
9: KNIT ROW: Bind off 1 stitch. Knit to end of row. Turn work.
10: PURL ROW: Purl 1 row. Turn work.
Repeat rows 9 and 10 2 (3, 3) more times.

• When you are done with the bind-off instructions, measure the length of the front piece, comparing it to the length of the back. If the back and front measure the same, bind off the remaining stitches. If the front is too short, continue knitting and purling until the pieces are of equal length, then bind off.

• Attach yarn to the other side of the hole and begin binding off 3 stitches immediately. You will now be binding off when you are purling. Finish neck shaping as for the other side and bind off.

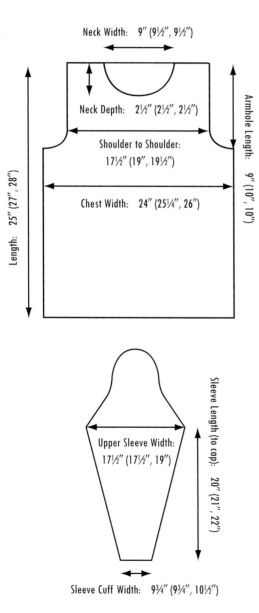

Neck Width: 9" (9½", 9½")

Neck Depth: 2½" (2½", 2½")

Armhole Length: 9" (10", 10")

Shoulder to Shoulder: 17½" (19", 19½")

Chest Width: 24" (25¼", 26")

Length: 25" (27", 28")

Upper Sleeve Width: 17½" (17½", 19")

Sleeve Length (to cap): 20" (21", 22")

Sleeve Cuff Width: 9¾" (9¾", 10½")

the Compromise

There is an adage in the knitting world that knitting a sweater for a prospective husband without a ring on your finger is bad luck. Old wives' tale or not, we've heard countless stories from women (and sometimes men) who knitted a sweater for their beloved and were dumped soon after. Despite our repeated warnings to prospective knitters (and brides), many choose not to heed our wisdom. We came up with this sweater as a compromise; it's such a quick and easy sweater to make, we figure that even if things don't work out, no blood, sweat, or tears were wasted. Kathleen made this sweater in two weeks, gave it to her boyfriend for his birthday, and a month later they broke up. She simply shrugged and laughed, saying at least the relationship had lasted a little longer than it took to make the sweater.

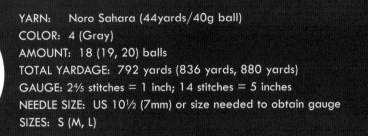

YARN: Noro Sahara (44yards/40g ball)
COLOR: 4 (Gray)
AMOUNT: 18 (19, 20) balls
TOTAL YARDAGE: 792 yards (836 yards, 880 yards)
GAUGE: 2⅘ stitches = 1 inch; 14 stitches = 5 inches
NEEDLE SIZE: US 10½ (7mm) or size needed to obtain gauge
SIZES: S (M, L)

back:

With #10½ needle cast on 68, (72, 74) stitches. Work in K2, P2 ribbing as follows: For Small & Medium: Work in K2, P2 ribbing for 3″. For Large: Row 1: K2, *(P2, K2)* to end. Row 2: P2, *(K2, P2)* to end. Repeat rows 1 & 2 for 3″. Then work in St st until piece measures 16″ (16½″, 18″) from cast-on edge, ending with a WS row. **SHAPE ARMHOLES:** Bind off 3 stitches at the beginning of the next 2 rows. Bind off 2 stitches at the beginning of the next 2 rows. Then decrease 1 stitch at each edge every other row 3 (2, 2) times, until 52 (58, 60) stitches remain. Continue to work in St st until piece measures 25″ (26½″, 28″) from cast-on edge. Bind off remaining stitches.

front:

Work as for back until piece measures 16″, (16½″, 18″). **SHAPE ARMHOLES AS FOR BACK.** Continue in St st until piece measures 22½″ (24″, 25½″) from cast-on edge, ending with a WS row. **SHAPE NECK:** Bind off center 10 stitches. Working each side of neck separately, at the beginning of each neck edge every other row bind off 3 stitches 1 times, 2 stitches 1 time, 1 stitch 1 (2, 2) times. Continue working in St st on remaining 15 (17, 18) stitches until piece measures same as back. Bind off remaining stitches.

sleeves:

With #10½ needle, cast on 30 (30, 30) stitches. Work in K2, P2 ribbing as follows: Row 1: K2 *(P2, K2)* to end. Row 2: P2 *(K2, P2)* to end. Repeat rows 1 & 2 for 3″. Work in St st. At the same time, increase 1 stitch at each edge every 6th row 9 (11, 11) times until you have 48 (52, 52) stitches. Continue in St st until sleeve measures 18″ (19″, 19½″). **NOTE:** Increase leaving 2 edge stitches on either side of work. This means you should knit 2 stitches, increase a stitch, knit to the last 2 stitches, increase a stitch, and then knit the remaining 2 stitches. Increasing like this makes it easier to sew up your seams. **SHAPE CAP:** Bind off 3 stitches at the beginning of the next 2 rows. Bind off 2 stitches at the beginning of the next 2 rows. Then decrease 1 stitch at each edge every other row 1 (2, 2) times. Bind off remaining 36 (38, 38) stitches.

finishing:

Sew shoulder seams together. Sew sleeves on. Sew side and sleeve seams. With a 10½ 16-inch circular needle, pick up 48 stitches around neck and work in K2, P2 ribbing for 8″. Bind off loosely.

STEP-BY-STEP GUIDE TO SHAPING THE ARMHOLE

1: KNIT ROW: Bind off 3 stitches, knit to end.
2: PURL ROW: Bind off 3 stitches, purl to end.
3: KNIT ROW: Bind off 2 stitches, knit to end.
4: PURL ROW: Bind off 2 stitches, purl to end.
5: KNIT ROW: Knit 1 stitch, K2tog, knit until 3 stitches remain on left needle, K2tog, K1.
6: PURL ROW: Purl.
Repeat rows 5 & 6 2 (1, 1) more times.

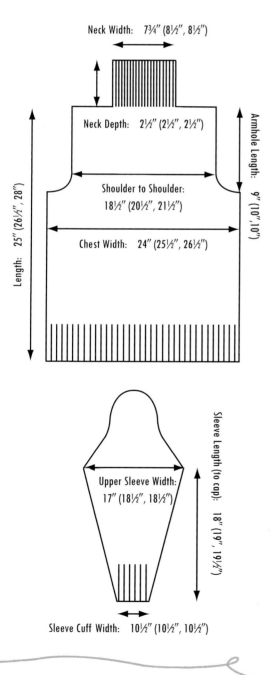

Neck Width: 7¾" (8½", 8½")

Neck Depth: 2½" (2½", 2½")

Armhole Length: 9" (10", 10")

Length: 25" (26½", 28")

Shoulder to Shoulder:
18½" (20½", 21½")

Chest Width: 24" (25½", 26½")

Upper Sleeve Width:
17" (18½", 18½")

Sleeve Length (to cap):   18" (19", 19½")

Sleeve Cuff Width: 10½" (10½", 10½")

STEP-BY-STEP GUIDE TO SHAPING THE NECK

A turtleneck is shaped just as a crewneck would be; the only difference is in the finishing. After you pick up stitches around the neck you'll knit 7 to 8 inches rather than just 1. Remember that after binding off the center stitches, you will work one side of the neck at a time. To bind off center stitches:

1: KNIT ROW: Knit 23 (26, 27) stitches; with the 22nd (25th, 26th) stitch begin to bind off the center 10 stitches. For example, for size Small, this means you should pull the 22nd stitch over the 23rd stitch. When you are done binding off the center, check to make sure you have 21 (24, 25) stitches on each side of the hole including the stitch on the right needle. Knit to end of row. Turn work.
2: PURL ROW: Purl 1 row. Turn work.
3: KNIT ROW: Bind off first 3 stitches. Knit to end of row. Turn work.
4: PURL ROW: Purl 1 row. Turn work.
5: KNIT ROW: Bind off first 2 stitches. Knit to end of row. Turn work.
6: PURL ROW: Purl 1 row. Turn work.
7: KNIT ROW: Bind off 1 stitch. Knit to end of row. Turn work.
8: PURL ROW: Purl 1 row. Turn work.
Repeat rows 7 & 8 0 (1, 1) more times.

• When you are done with the bind-off instructions, measure the length of the front piece, comparing it to the length of the back. If the front and back measure the same, bind off the remaining stitches. If the front is too short, continue knitting and purling until the pieces are of equal length, then bind off.

• Attach yarn to the other side of the neck edge and begin binding off 3 stitches immediately. You will now be binding off when you are purling. Finish neck shaping as for the other side and bind off.

the exception to the rule

We know, we know, we said, "Don't knit a sweater for your boyfriend until you have a big fat diamond." Julie disobeyed her own sage advice and knitted this sweater for her then boyfriend, John, and it turned out to be the exception to a generally sound rule. Before she knitted it, she made him swear that if he broke up with her, he'd give the sweater back. John thought that was a pretty good deal; if he ever did want to break up with her, he reasoned, he could just hand her the sweater instead of worrying about how to let her down easy. Luckily for everyone, he handed her a ring instead.

YARN: Grignasco Top Print (110 yards /50g ball)
COLOR: 76
AMOUNT: 18 (19, 20) balls
TOTAL YARDAGE: 1,980 yards (2,090 yards, 2,200 yards)
GAUGE: 4 stitches = 1 inch
NEEDLE SIZE: US 9 (5½mm) or size needed to obtain gauge
SIZES: S (M, L)

Yarn is worked doubled throughout sweater—this means you should hold 2 strands of yarn together as though they are 1.

back:

With #9 needle and 2 strands of yarn, cast on 96 (100, 104) stitches. Work in K2, P2 ribbing for 2″. Then work in St st until piece measures 16″ (16½″, 17″) from cast-on edge. **SHAPE ARMHOLES:** Bind off 4 stitches at the beginning of the next 2 rows. Bind off 3 stitches at the beginning of the next 2 rows. Bind off 2 stitches at the beginning of the next 2 rows. Then decrease 1 stitch at each end every other row 2 (3, 4) times until 74 (76, 78) stitches remain. Continue in St st until piece measures 25″ (26½″, 27″) from cast-on edge. Bind off remaining stitches.

front:

Work as for back until piece measures 16″ (16½″, 17″). **SHAPE ARMHOLES AS FOR BACK.** Continue in St st until piece measures 17″ (18½″, 19″) from cast-on edge, ending on a WS row. **SHAPE V-NECK:** Place a marker around needle in center of work (see page 50), then shape as follows: Row 1: Knit to 4 stitches before the marker, K2, K2tog. Turn work. Row 2: Purl. Repeat rows 1 & 2 9 (9, 10) more times until 27 (28, 28) stitches remain. Then work as follows: Row 1: Knit to 4 stitches before the marker, K2, K2tog. Row 2: Purl. Row 3: Knit. Row 4: Purl. Repeat these 4 rows 4 more times until 22 (23, 23) stitches remain. When piece measures same as back, bind off remaining stitches. Attach yarn to remaining stitches and shape V as follows: Row 1: K2, SSK, knit to end of row. Row 2: Purl. Repeat rows 1 & 2 9 (9, 10) more times until 27 (28, 28) stitches remain. Then work as follows: Row 1: K2, SSK, knit to end of row. Row 2: Purl. Row 3: Knit. Row 4: Purl. Repeat these 4 rows 4 more times until 22 (23, 23) stitches remain. Work until piece measures same as back. Bind off remaining stitches. **NOTE:** K2tog = knit 2 stitches together. SSK (slip, slip, knit) = slip 2 stitches onto right needle as if to knit them, insert left needle into front of stitches, and knit the 2 stitches together.

sleeves:

With #9 needle and 2 strands of yarn, cast on 36 (40, 40) stitches. Work in K2, P2 ribbing for 2″. Then work in St st. At the same time, increase 1 stitch at each edge every 4th row 15 (17, 17) times until you have 66 (74, 74) stitches. Continue in St st until sleeve measures 17″ (18″, 19½″). **NOTE:** Increase leaving 2 edge stitches on either side of work. This means you should knit 2 stitches, increase a stitch, knit to the last 2 stitches, increase a stitch, and then knit the remaining 2 stitches. Increasing like this makes it easier to sew up your seams. **SHAPE CAP:** Bind off 4 stitches at the beginning of the next 2 rows. Bind off 3 stitches at the beginning of the next 2 rows. Bind off 2 stitches at the beginning of the following 2 rows. Then decrease 1 stitch at each end every other row 2 (3, 3) times. Bind off remaining 44 (50, 50) stitches.

finishing:

Sew shoulder seams together. Sew sleeves on. Sew side and sleeve seams. With #9 circular 24″ needle starting at right back neck, pick up 30 stitches across back neck, pick up 38 stitches down left front, place a marker, pick up 2 stitches, place a marker, pick up 38 stitches up right front. Work in K2, P2, rib for 6 rows as follows. K2, P2 until 2 Sts before marker, SSk, slip marker onto right needle, K2. Slip marker onto right needle, K2tog. Then begin P2, K2 up right front. Repeat this for 6 rows then bind off loosely.

STEP-BY-STEP GUIDE TO SHAPING THE ARMHOLE

1: KNIT ROW: Bind off 4 stitches, knit to end.
2: PURL ROW: Bind off 4 stitches, purl to end.
3: KNIT ROW: Bind off 3 stitches, knit to end.
4: PURL ROW: Bind off 3 stitches, purl to end.
5: KNIT ROW: Bind off 2 stitches, knit to end.
6: PURL ROW: Bind off 2 stitches, purl to end.
7: KNIT ROW: Knit 1 stitch, K2tog, knit until 3 stitches remain on left needle, K2tog, K1.
8: PURL ROW: Purl.
   Repeat rows 7 & 8 1 (2, 3) more times.

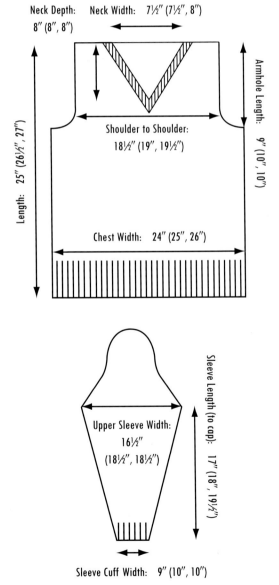

Neck Depth: 8″ (8″, 8″)

Neck Width: 7½″ (7½″, 8″)

Armhole Length: 9″ (10″, 10″)

Shoulder to Shoulder: 18½″ (19″, 19½″)

Length: 25″ (26½″, 27″)

Chest Width: 24″ (25″, 26″)

Upper Sleeve Width: 16½″ (18½″, 18½″)

Sleeve Length (to cap): 17″ (18″, 19½″)

Sleeve Cuff Width: 9″ (10″, 10″)

First you must place a marker around the needle in the center of the work.

LEFT SHAPING (left side when worn)
1: KNIT ROW: Knit to 4 stitches before the marker, K2tog, K2.
2: PURL ROW: Purl.
Repeat rows 1 & 2 9 (9,10) more times. Then work as follows:
1: KNIT ROW: Knit to 4 stitches before the marker, K2tog, K2.
2: PURL ROW: Purl.
3: KNIT ROW: Knit.
4: PURL ROW: Purl.
Repeat rows 1–4 4 (4, 4) more times.
Attach yarn to other side of V.

• When you are done with the bind-off instructions, measure the length of the front piece, comparing it to the length of the back. If the front and back measure the same, bind off the remaining stitches. If the front is too short, continue knitting and purling until the pieces are of equal length, then bind off.

RIGHT SHAPING (right side when worn)
1: KNIT ROW: K2, SSK, knit to end of row.
2: PURL ROW: Purl.
Repeat rows 1 & 2 9 (9, 10) more times. Then work as follows:
1: KNIT ROW: K2, SSK, knit to end of row.
2: PURL ROW: Purl.
3: KNIT ROW: Knit.
4: PURL ROW: Purl.
Repeat rows 1–4 4 (4, 4) more times.

Hats

Hats are generally the quickest and smallest projects you can make. Even though hats knit up lickety-split, they can be a great introduction to techniques such as decreasing, stripes, ribbing, and sewing up a seam. We're sure that once you've polished off a few of these snappy little numbers you'll want to apply those newly honed knitting skills to more ambitious projects.

Jeff's Sporty Striped Hat is very easy because it's knit in the round, so all you do is knit—no purling required. It also introduces the idea of adding stripes. *The Knitting Club's Hat* is also done in all knit but it looks entirely different from *Jeff's Hat* because it's worked back and forth, knitting over knit rows, which creates a bumpy texture. *Feeling Fuzzy* has a ribbing at the bottom and is done in stockinette stitch. All these hats are so fast and easy, you'll want to have one to go with every coat in your closet.

jeff's striped hat

This hat is made on round needles, so all you have to do is knit, no purling. And because it is knit in a circle, there are no seams to sew when you are done. In fact, it is such a cinch that even Jordana's husband, Jeff, made one. You can be a little zany with this hat and play with the colors and the stripe patterns in any way you want. Jeff is a big sports fan, so Jordana made him one with thin navy and white Yankee pinstripes, and another with wide red and blue Rangers stripes. (She was going to complete the trilogy and make him an orange- and-blue Knicks hat, too, but Jeff was afraid people might mistake him for a Mets fan.)

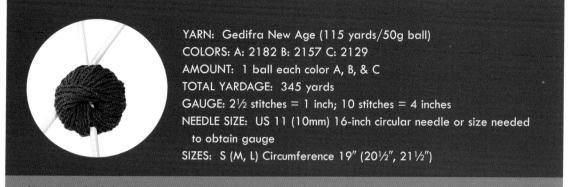

YARN: Gedifra New Age (115 yards/50g ball)
COLORS: A: 2182 B: 2157 C: 2129
AMOUNT: 1 ball each color A, B, & C
TOTAL YARDAGE: 345 yards
GAUGE: 2½ stitches = 1 inch; 10 stitches = 4 inches
NEEDLE SIZE: US 11 (10mm) 16-inch circular needle or size needed
   to obtain gauge
SIZES: S (M, L) Circumference 19″ (20½″, 21½″)

Yarn is worked doubled throughout the hat—this means you should hold 2 strands of yarn together as though they are 1.

NOTE: Changing colors is just like starting a new ball of yarn. All you need to do is attach the new color to the end of the old color with a simple double knot. Leave ends on both colors long enough to weave them in at the end (about 3–4″). If you are going to stripe two colors several times, just attach the second color without cutting the first and work while both colors are attached, picking up the colors as you need them. With #11 circular needle and 2 strands of color A, cast on 48 (52, 54) stitches. Place a marker at the beginning of your row and join stitches in a circle. Make sure all stitches are facing the same way and that you are not twisting them. Work in St

st (knitting each round) for 4″. Cut color A and attach color B. Work in St st for 2″. Cut color B and attach color C. Work in St st for 1¼″. Begin to decrease as follows:

Row 1: *K4, K2tog* 8 times, end K2.
Row 2: *K3, K2tog* 8 times, end K2.
Row 3: *K2, K2tog* 8 times, end K2.
Row 4: *K1, K2tog* 8 times, end K2.
Cut yarn, leaving an 8″ tail. With a yarn needle, thread the yarn tail through the remaining loops on the needle and pull until the top of the hat is closed. Pull the remaining yarn through to the WS of work and secure it.

the knitting club's hat

Trish is a junior high school teacher who started an afterschool knitting club for her students. A few months earlier, she had come to our store and decided on this pattern. She loved the way it came out, and her girls were always complimenting her on it, so she arranged a field trip to the store. Each girl picked out a different shade of the Koigu wool. Even though they're making the same hat, each one will look unique because this wool comes in so many beautiful color combinations. The hat would also look great in a solid color, just a little more conservative.

YARN: Koigu (175 yards/50g ball)
COLOR: P800
AMOUNT: 2 balls
TOTAL YARDAGE: 350 yards
GAUGE: 4 stitches = 1″; 16 stitches = 4 inches
NEEDLE SIZE: US 9 (5.5 mm) or size needed to obtain gauge
SIZES: S, (M, L) Circumference: 18″ (20″, 22″)

Yarn is worked doubled throughout the hat—this means you should hold 2 strands of yarn together as though they are 1.

With #9 needle and 2 strands of yarn cast on 72 (80, 88) stitches. Work in garter (all knit) until piece measures 6½″ (7″, 7½″) from cast on edge, ending on a WS row. Then work as follows:

Row 1: *K5, K2tog* across row.
Rows 2, 4, 6, 8, & 10: Knit.
Row 3: *K4, K2tog* across row.
Row 5: *K3, K2tog* across row.
Row 7: *K2, K2tog* across row.
Row 9: *K1, K2tog* across row.
Row 11: *K2tog* across row.

Cut yarn leaving a 12″ tail. With a yarn needle, thread the yarn tail through the remaining loops on the needle. Sew seam of hat on RS until 2″ remain, put yarn through to WS, and sew remaining 2″ on the wrong side of the hat. This is done so you can't see a seam when you fold up the brim of the hat.

feeling fuzzy

Everyone needs a basic hat. Everyone wants a basic hat. In fact, if we could name the most often requested pattern among our customers it would be—you guessed it—a basic hat. Well, search no more. This is, without a doubt, the epitome of standard, everyday, all-purpose hats. Its ribbed bottom folds up to make a cuff, and it fits tight to the head, kind of like a fisherman's cap. The yarn we used is so soft and fuzzy, it will keep you warm on even the coldest of days.

YARN: GGH Soft Kid (145 yards/25g ball)
COLOR: #54 (Apple Green)
AMOUNT: 3 balls
TOTAL YARDAGE: 435 yards
GAUGE: 3⅓ stitches = 1"; 18 stitches = 5 inches
NEEDLE SIZES: US 10½ (7mm) for body of hat & US 9
    (5½mm) for ribbing or sizes needed to obtain gauge
SIZES: S, (M, L) Circumference: 18" (20", 22")

Yarn is worked tripled throughout hat—this means you should hold 3 strands of yarn together as though they are 1.

With #9 needle and 3 strands of yarn, cast on 60 (66, 72) stitches. Work in K3, P3 ribbing for 4". Change to #10½ needle and work in St st until piece measures 7½" (7¾", 8") from cast-on edge, ending on a WS row. Then work as follows:
Row 1: *K5, K2tog* across row.
Rows 2,4,6,8, & 10: Purl.
Row 3: *K4, K2tog* across row.
Row 5: *K3, K2tog* across row.
Row 7: *K2, K2tog* across row.
Row 9: *K1, K2tog* across row.
Row 11: *K2tog* across row.

Cut yarn leaving 12" tail. With a yarn needle, thread the yarn tail through the remaining loops on the needle. Sew seam of hat on RS until 2" remain, put yarn through to wrong side and sew remaining 2" on the WS, of the hat. This is done so you can't see a seam when you fold up the brim of the hat.

Scarves

We'd have to vote scarves the least intimidating and most popular beginner project. Making a scarf is a quick, manageable undertaking that involves no shaping of armholes or necks and no sewing anything together. Hey, it's just one long strip, a piece of cake, right? Still feeling intimidated? Well guess what—scarves look great in garter stitch, which means you can just knit every row. (That way if you put your work down you don't have to worry if it's a knit or purl row.) Scarves can also be knit in stockinette stitch to practice your knitting and purling prowess before tackling a whole sweater. Do note that scarves knit in stockinette stitch can curl at the edges; it's just the nature of the stitch and there's nothing you can do about it. *The Chunkiest of the Chunky* is knit in garter stitch on big needles. It is certainly the fastest and easiest project in this book and great for the knitter who wants to master 1 stitch at a time. *Hole in One* and *Airy Wrap* are both knit in stockinette stitch and curl, but that's the look we wanted. Both of these scarves are a snap, so think about making extras as gifts. Because they don't require balls and balls of wool, go ahead and indulge your passion for the finer things with a luxurious silk, angora, or cashmere blend yarn for extra-cozy necks all winter.

hole-in-one

You don't have to be

Tiger Woods to knit this scarf. We have to admit we stole the idea from a two-year-old named Olivia who came into the store one day with her mom wearing a neck wrap like this one. The scarf is small, so it doesn't get in the way or add bulk, but it's warm and stylish for any age. We loved the design so much that we created our own, choosing a luxurious hand-dyed angora. Since it takes only one skein and knits up in no time, we've made tons of these scarves as gifts. Do explain that the hole is there on purpose; it allows the wearer to pull one end through so the scarf fits snugly around her neck.

YARN: Prism Angora (90 yards/ 1oz. ball)
COLOR: Lipstick
AMOUNT: 1 ball
TOTAL YARDAGE: 90 yards
GAUGE: 3.6 stitches = 1 inch;
   18 stitches = 5 inches
NEEDLE SIZE: US 10½ (7mm)
   or size needed to obtain gauge
SIZES: One size

instructions:

With #10½ needle cast on 25 stitches. Work in St st for 5″. Then make the hole: K11, K2tog, yo, K12. Continue in St st until approximately 24″ of yarn remain. Bind off.

airy wrap

This being New York, we get all kinds of customers—even the odd celebrity or two. While we won't name names, we will tell you that this scarf was inspired by a storebought item worn by one of our more recognizable customers. We liked its airy look, as well as the contrasting texture of the fringe. Our version is made with a doubled strand of Thais; it's made from Kid Mohair, a very warm, light, and soft fiber.

Yarn is worked doubled throughout the scarf—this means you should hold 2 strands of yarn together as though they are 1.

YARN: Lang Thais (125 yards/ 25g ball); Lang Mystic (165 yards/25g ball)
COLOR: Thais # 4791 (purple); Mystic #1— (purple)
AMOUNT: 8 balls Thais; 1 ball Mystic
TOTAL YARDAGE: 1,000 yards
GAUGE: 2 stitches = 1 inch; 8 stitches = 4 inches
NEEDLE SIZE: US 15 (10mm) or size needed to obtain gauge
SIZES: One size

Yarn is worked doubled throughout the scarf—this means you should hold 2 strands of yarn together as though they are 1.

instructions:

With #15 needle and 2 strands of yarn, cast on 44 stitches. Work in St st until piece measures 76". Bind off loosely. Make fringe with Mystic and Thais and place as desired.

the chunkiest of the chunky

Jordana recently spent some time with two young relatives who wanted to learn to knit. She brought a huge bag of yarn and hefty size 35 needles and in two days eight-year-old Erica produced this great chunky scarf. Big needles make the scarf knit like lightning and give it a very soft feel. P.S.: Not long afterward, we saw a similar scarf on Madison Avenue selling for $150.

YARN: Horstia Marokko (88 yards/200g ball)
COLOR: #100
AMOUNT: 2 balls
TOTAL YARDAGE: 176 yards
GAUGE: 1 stitch = 1 inch
NEEDLE SIZE: US 35 (20mm)
   or size needed to obtain gauge
SIZES: One size

instructions:

With #35 needle, cast on 12 stitches. Work in garter stitch (knit every row) until piece measures 60″. Bind off loosely. Make fringe and place as desired.

Ponchos

Remember ponchos? We bet if you look back through your family photos circa 1972 you'll find one of yourself, happily enshrouded in one of these carefree coverups. Well, ponchos are back and they are a fun project for all knitters. Two of the ponchos in this chapter are done in garter stitch (which means no purling) and use increasing and decreasing techniques. *Rectangles Only* is made from two rectangles that are sewn together. We did ours in stockinette stitch and trimmed it with a fancy edging, but you could certainly try out a different stitch here if you want, a rib or seed stitch maybe. *Easy, Breezy, Beautiful . . .* is a summer poncho, done in cotton yarns. *Winter Poncho* is meant for crisper days—it is made in a mixture of heavier yarns and knit on a much bigger needle. The interesting thing about these two ponchos is that the instructions are almost the same but the sizes of the ponchos are dramatically different. See, gauge does matter.

easy, breezy, beautiful

Jordana was invited to a seaside wedding that was to take place in late May. It gets cool at night at the beach so Jordana thought she would whip up a shawl to go with her new dress. Halfway through, she remembered how annoying shawls can be, always needing to be rewrapped and never staying in place. Her next thought was to make a cardigan, but time was running out. Then in walked a customer who had made our winter poncho, and inspiration struck: Jordana would make a summer version of our winter poncho. It took her less than three days, and she got almost as many compliments as the bride.

YARN: Berroco Metallica (85 yards/50g ball) and Klaus Koch
Kollection Clip (175 yards/100g ball)
COLOR: Metallica 1009; Klaus Koch Kollektion Clip 133
AMOUNT: 4 balls Metallica, 2 balls Clip
TOTAL YARDAGE: 340 yards Metallica; 350 yards Clip
GAUGE: 3 stitches = 1 inch; 12 stitches = 4 inches
NEEDLE SIZE: US 13 (9mm) or size needed to obtain gauge
SIZES: One size

Yarn is worked doubled throughout the poncho—this means you should hold 1 strand of color A and 1 strand of color B together as though they are 1.
INCREASE: Knit into the front and the back of the first and last stitch on each row.
DECREASE: K2, K2 together.

back:

With #13 needle and 1 strand of each yarn, cast on 2 stitches. Increase 1 stitch at each edge every row until you have 72 stitches. Then begin decreasing 1 stitch at the beginning only of each row until 24 stitches remain.

front:

Work as for back, increasing up to 72 stitches and decreasing until piece measures 3½" less than back. **SHAPE NECK:** Bind off center 4 stitches. Working each side of neck separately, at each neck edge, every decrease 1 stitch 6 times. Continue working until piece measures same as back. NOTE: Remember to keep decreasing at side edge also. You should have 6 stitches when you are binding off.

finishing:

Sew front and back of poncho together from the shoulder down the entire decreased edge. With 9mm (N) crochet hook and 1 strand of each yarn held together, work 1 row of single crochet and 1 row of shrimp stitch around neck edge. Make fringe using 2 strands of each yarn, and attach it, spacing it evenly around the poncho at intervals of approximately 1 inch.

winter poncho

This poncho is inspired by an old-fashioned "little girl's" poncho. The original pattern was from the 1960s or maybe the 1970s. (We're young enough to be able to call 60s' fashions "old-fashioned.") That poncho was worked on small needles and with very traditional yarns, but we overhauled the pattern to update the style, combining a bunch of funky yarns and knitting them on a size 19 needle. Dozens of our customers have made this poncho, and every one was an original because each knitter picked her own combinations of textures and colors. Heather mixed red mohair with dark gray wool, Deena mixed three different shades of black, and Guggie combined lavender mohair with deep purple wool. Each one was amazing! Be sure to have fun with your yarn combinations when you knit this project, and don't be afraid to experiment a little. This is a great beginner project because all you have to do is knit, and you'll learn increases and decreases along the way.

YARN: Manos Del Uruguay (135 yards/100g ball), and GGH
  Mohair 2000 (160 yards/50g ball), Filatura Di Crosa Redox (154
  yards/50g ball)
COLOR: Manos: Color C; Mohair 2000: Color 52; Redox: Color 4
AMOUNT: Manos: 5 skeins; Mohair 2000: 5skeins; Redox: 5 skeins
TOTAL YARDAGE: Manos: 675 yards, Mohair 2000: 800 yards,
  Redox: 770 yards
GAUGE: 2 stitches= 1 inch; 8 stitches = 4 inches
NEEDLE SIZE: US 19 (15mm) for body & US 13 (8½mm) for ribbing
  or sizes needed to obtain gauge
SIZES: One size

Yarns are worked tripled throughout the poncho—this means you should hold 1 strand of yarn A, 1
one strand of yarn B, and 1 strand of yarn C together as though they are 1.
INCREASE: Knit into the front and the back of the first and last stitch on each row.
DECREASE: K2, K2 together.

back & front (make 2):

With #19 needle and 1 strand of each color yarn, cast on 2 stitches. Increase 1 stitch at each edge every row until you have 72 stitches. Then begin decreasing 1 stitch at the beginning only of each row 22 times, until 50 stitches remain. Then decrease 1 stitch at each end of every row 18 times until 16 stitches remain. Change to #13 needle and work in K1, P1 ribbing for 4″. Bind off very loosely.

finishing:

Sew front and back of poncho together from the neck down the entire decreased edge. Make fringe, using 2 strands of each yarn held together, and attach it, spacing it out evenly around the poncho at intervals of approximately 2 inches.

rectangles only

Last fall we were doing our annual "shopping tour" of Manhattan's upscale stores when we spotted an itsy bitsy angora poncho in a baby department. When we inspected it, we realized it was just two rectangles sewn together in a peculiar way. We immediately went back to the store and knitted one in a grown-up size. Eureka! This is a great beginner project because it is just two stockinette rectangles and the pattern can be adapted easily for any yarn.

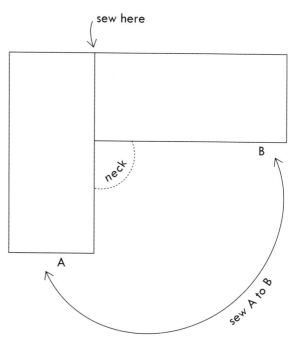

YARN: Noro Cashiroha (99 yards/40g ball); Muench Touch Me
(61 yards/50g ball)
COLORS: Cashiroha: #42 & #44; Touch Me: #3623
AMOUNT: 12 balls Cashiroha (6 in each color); 2 balls Touch Me
TOTAL YARDAGE: 1,188 yards Cashiroha; 122 yards Touch Me
GAUGE: 3 stitches = 1"; 12 stitches = 4 inches
NEEDLE SIZE: US 11 (8mm) or size needed to obtain gauge
FINISHED MEASUREMENTS: 18" × 28"

Yarn is worked doubled throughout the poncho—this means you should hold 1 strand of color A and 1 strand of color B together as though they are 1.

rectangles: (make 2)

With #11 needle and 1 strand of each color of Cashiroha yarn, cast on 54 stitches. Work in St st until piece measures 28". Bind off.

finishing:

Sew together as shown in diagram below. Make 4 large tassels out of Touch Me yarn. Attach 1 tassel at each point on the front and back. Then attach 1 tassel at each side.

how to make tassel:

Cut a piece of cardboard approximately 6" long. Wrap the Touch Me yarn 20 times around the length of cardboard. Cut a piece of yarn about 18" long and threaded double onto a tapestry needle. Insert the needle under all strands at the upper edge of cardboard. Pull tightly and knot securely near strands. Cut the yarn loops at the lower edge of the cardboard. Cut a piece of yarn about 12" long and wrap tightly around loops about 1½" below the top knot to form tassel neck. Knot securely and pull the ends to center of tassel.

sew here

neck

A

B

sew A to B

Throws

Throws sometimes seem a bit scary to new knitters because they are big. Their size is undeniable, but if you think of them as just supersized scarves, maybe you'll find them easier to manage. Throws are great because they require no shaping, so you don't have to worry about increasing and decreasing. And you never have to worry about fit. If the throw is a little wider or longer than you expected, you can just shrug your shoulders and say, "Oh well." This is not, however, license to skip that all-important gauge swatch step. Always means always!

The three throws here are all extremely straightforward. *Bulky Blanket* defines easy. It is done in garter stitch—each row is knit—and involves no sewing, although it does require that you follow a simple stripe pattern, and when you're done there are a number of ends to weave in. *Design Your Own Throw* is probably the simplest and most fun project in this group because there is no real pattern to follow, there are no ends to weave in, and you can just play with color and texture and knit away. *How Deena Got her Ooohs and Aaahs* is the most advanced, but it's still definitely a manageable project for any beginner. It is done in stockinette stitch and has a very precise (yet random) stripe pattern. Because it is knit in strips, you will also get a bit of sewing practice.

bulky blanket

We created this pattern when Angela wanted to knit a chenille throw for the end of her bed. We spent a lot of time knitting swatches in different color combinations with different striping patterns before we finally came up with this pattern. Angela, whose blanket is knit with a single strand of chenille, was still working on it last we checked; this version made with doubled yarn, knits up much faster. Angela, we hate to say it, but we told you that you should have doubled the yarn!

YARN: Crystal Palace Chenille (98 yards/50g ball)
COLORS: A: 4519, B: 3409, C: 6885, D: 3777
AMOUNT: A: 8 skeins, B: 12 skeins, C: 8 skeins, D: 2 skeins
YARDAGE: Color A: 800 yards; Color B: 1200 yards; Color C: 800 yards; Color D: 200 yards
GAUGE: 3 stitches = 1 inch; 12 stitches = 4 inches
NEEDLE SIZE: US 11 (8mm) 32-inch circular or size needed to obtain gauge
FINISHED MEASUREMENTS: 40″ × 52″

Yarn is worked doubled throughout the blanket—this means you should hold 2 strands of the color you are working with together as though they are 1.

instructions:

With #11 32-inch circular needle and 2 strands of yarn, cast on 120 stitches.
Working in garter stitch (all knit) work as follows:

8 rows color A

6 rows color B

4 rows color C

2 rows color D

4 rows color C

6 rows color B

Repeat this pattern a total of 10 times. Work 8 rows of A. Bind off all stitches loosely.

finishing:

At side edges, with a size J crochet hook and 2 strands color A yarn, work 1 row of single crochet and 1 row of shrimp stitch.

design your own throw

Picking out the yarn for this blanket is as much fun as knitting it. It's a great opportunity to play with color and texture without regard to gauge. In other words, there are no rules and no limitations—you can use any yarn you want. We like to begin by picking a color scheme, green in this case. We pull out every green yarn in the store and make a huge pile on the floor. You should do the same. Pick a color and then walk around your yarn shop gathering different yarns (your local yarn shop owner will love the mess this makes!).

Although there are no rules, we do have a few pointers that may help you in picking out your yarns:

- Choose approximately 15–20 different yarns of varying shade and texture.
- Use a few yarns that contain mohair. They add depth, body, and fluff to your throw.
- Use some metallic or glittery yarn. It will add life to the blanket. Even if you aren't a fan of the glitzy yarns, a row here and there really adds dimension and interest.
- Use your imagination. Do not leave out a yarn because you don't like it. Remember, you use it only one row at a time and it will be scattered throughout the blanket. Focus on the texture and color that it may add to the overall picture.

YARN: Assorted
TOTAL YARDAGE: Approximately 1,800 yards
GAUGE: Approximately 2½ stitches = 1 inch; 10 stitches = 4 inches
NEEDLE SIZE: US 11 (8mm) 32-inch circular
FINISHED MEASUREMENTS: 40" × 60"

Note: Although this project is knitted on circular needles, it is NOT knitted in the round. The circular needles can accommodate the large number of stitches required for the throw, but you must still knit back and forth to create the garter stitch; otherwise you will create a long tube!

instructions:

With #11 32-inch circular needle, cast on 150 stitches. Work in garter stitch (all knit), using a new yarn for each row. You can pick up the yarn in a random way—close your eyes, reach in your bag, and leave it to fate—or set up a pattern. Leave 4"–6" ends at the beginning and end of each row. These ends will be used as part of your fringe. Knit until the blanket measures approximately 40" (this is the width; you are knitting the blanket lengthwise). Bind off loosely.

finishing:

Make 4"–6" inch strands of fringe with the leftover yarn and attach it to the ends of the blanket. The fringe should be placed close together, giving it a thick, plush look.

how deena got her oohs and aaahs

Deena wanted to make a blanket for a close friend's bridal shower. She wanted to hear oohs and aahs when her gift was opened and she wanted a project that *looked* complicated but would actually be fun and easy to knit. This throw met all her criteria, a simple stockinette blanket with asymmetrical striping. It's made in three strips so it's easier to work on and carry around, and it's a blast to make. And by the way, Deena definitely got her oohs and aahs! So will you.

YARN: Manos Del Uruguay
  (135 yards/100g ball)

COLORS:		AMOUNTS:
A	#18	1 skein
B	#29	1 skein
C	#D	1 skein
D	#24	1 skein
E	#26	2 skeins
F	#49	2 skeins
G	#A	1 skein
H	#M	2 skeins
I	#V	2 skeins
J	#32	1 skein

TOTAL YARDAGE: 1,890 yards
GAUGE: 4 stitches = 1 inch
  (16 stitches = 4 inches)
NEEDLE SIZE: US 9 (5½mm)
  or size needed to obtain
  gauge
FINISHED MEASUREMENTS:
  40" × 60"

Strip 1:

With #9 needle and color I, cast on 56 stitches. Work 6 rows in St st and continue as follows:

Color F	6 rows	Color C	2 rows
Color I	6 rows	Color J	2 rows
Color H	6 rows	Color C	2 rows
Color J	6 rows	Color J	2 rows
Color H	6 rows	Color C	2 rows
Color E	6 rows	Color B	8 rows
Color I	6 rows	Color D	8 rows
Color C	6 rows	Color F	8 rows
Color J	6 rows	Color I	8 rows
Color A	6 rows	Color H	8 rows
Color D	6 rows	Color G	8 rows
Color B	2 rows	Color H	2 rows
Color J	2 rows	Color G	2 rows
Color B	2 rows	Color I	2 rows
Color J	2 rows	Color G	2 rows
Color B	2 rows	Color F	2 rows
Color J	2 rows	Color G	2 rows
Color B	2 rows	Color J	2 rows
Color J	2 rows	Color G	2 rows
Color B	2 rows	Color D	2 rows
Color J	2 rows	Color A	6 rows
Color H	2 rows	Color J	6 rows
Color J	2 rows	Color C	6 rows
Color H	2 rows	Color I	6 rows
Color J	2 rows	Color E	6 rows
Color H	4 rows	Color H	6 rows
Color I	4 rows	Color J	6 rows
Color F	4 rows	Color H	6 rows
Color H	4 rows	Color I	6 rows
Color I	4 rows	Color F	6 rows
Color F	4 rows	Color I	6 rows
Color H	4 rows		
Color I	4 rows		
Color F	4 rows		
Color H	4 rows		
Color I	4 rows		
Color F	2 rows		
Color E	2 rows		
Color F	2 rows		
Color E	2 rows		
Color F	2 rows		
Color E	2 rows		
Color J	2 rows		
Color E	2 rows		
Color J	2 rows		
Color C	2 rows		
Color J	2 rows		

Strip 2:

With #9 needle and color E, cast on 56 stitches. Work 6 rows in St st and continue as follows:

Color C	6 rows	Color F	2 rows
Color E	6 rows	Color B	2 rows
Color G	6 rows	Color F	2 rows
Color B	6 rows	Color B	2 rows
Color G	6 rows	Color F	2 rows
Color I	6 rows	Color D	8 rows
Color E	6 rows	Color A	8 rows
Color F	6 rows	Color C	8 rows
Color B	6 rows	Color E	8 rows
Color D	6 rows	Color G	8 rows
Color A	6 rows	Color H	8 rows
Color D	2 rows	Color G	2 rows
Color A	2 rows	Color H	2 rows
Color D	2 rows	Color E	2 rows
Color A	2 rows	Color H	2 rows
Color D	2 rows	Color C	2 rows
Color A	2 rows	Color H	2 rows
Color D	2 rows	Color A	2 rows
Color A	2 rows	Color H	2 rows
Color D	2 rows	Color B	2 rows
Color A	2 rows	Color D	6 rows
Color G	2 rows	Color B	6 rows
Color A	2 rows	Color F	6 rows
Color G	2 rows	Color E	6 rows
Color A	2 rows	Color I	6 rows
Color G	4 rows	Color G	6 rows
Color E	4 rows	Color B	6 rows
Color C	4 rows	Color G	6 rows
Color G	4 rows	Color E	6 rows
Color E	4 rows	Color C	6 rows
Color C	4 rows	Color E	6 rows
Color G	4 rows		
Color E	4 rows		
Color C	4 rows		
Color G	4 rows		
Color E	4 rows		
Color C	2 rows		
Color I	2 rows		
Color C	2 rows		
Color I	2 rows		
Color C	2 rows		
Color I	2 rows		
Color C	2 rows		
Color F	2 rows		
Color C	2 rows		
Color F	2 rows		
Color B	2 rows		

Strip 3:

With #9 needle and color H, cast on 56 stitches. Work 6 rows in St st and continue as follows:

Color F	6 rows	Color D	2 rows
Color H	6 rows	Color F	2 rows
Color I	6 rows	Color H	2 rows
Color C	6 rows	Color A	2 rows
Color I	6 rows	Color I	2 rows
Color J	6 rows	Color A	2 rows
Color G	6 rows	Color I	2 rows
Color F	6 rows	Color A	2 rows
Color D	6 rows	Color I	2 rows
Color B	6 rows	Color A	2 rows
Color J	6 rows	Color I	2 rows
Color B	2 rows	Color A	2 rows
Color C	2 rows	Color I	2 rows
Color B	2 rows	Color A	8 rows
Color C	2 rows	Color J	8 rows
Color B	2 rows	Color F	8 rows
Color C	2 rows	Color I	8 rows
Color B	2 rows	Color H	8 rows
Color C	2 rows	Color E	8 rows
Color B	2 rows	Color H	2 rows
Color C	2 rows	Color E	2 rows
Color B	2 rows	Color I	2 rows
Color E	2 rows	Color E	2 rows
Color B	2 rows	Color F	2 rows
Color E	2 rows	Color E	2 rows
Color H	4 rows	Color J	2 rows
Color E	4 rows	Color E	2 rows
Color F	4 rows	Color D	2 rows
Color H	4 rows	Color B	6 rows
Color E	4 rows	Color D	6 rows
Color F	4 rows	Color F	6 rows
Color H	4 rows	Color G	6 rows
Color E	4 rows	Color J	6 rows
Color F	2 rows	Color I	6 rows
Color H	2 rows	Color C	6 rows
Color F	2 rows	Color I	6 rows
		Color H	6 rows
		Color F	6 rows
		Color H	6 rows

finishing:

Work one row in single crochet around edges with colors F, I & H.

resources

Yarns used in this book can be ordered directly

through The Yarn Company. However, yarns change seasonally and it is possible that some of the yarns may not be available when you're ready to place an order. Be flexible; you don't have to use the exact yarns used in a given pattern in order to get a great result. Just choose a yarn or a combination of yarns that get the required gauge. You can also contact the manufacturer for local dealers; many have helpful websites with this type of information.

The following is a list of all the manufacturers whose yarns were used in this book:

THE YARN CO.
2274 Broadway
New York, NY 10024
(212) 787-7878
theyarnco.com

Lang and Berroco Yarns
BERROCO, INC.
Elmdale Road PO Box 367
Uxbridge, MA 01569
(800) 343-4948

Classic Elite Yarns
CLASSIC ELITE
300 Jackson Street
Lowell, MA 01852
(800) 343-0308

Crystal Palace Yarns
CRYSTAL PALACE
3006 San Pablo Avenue
Berkeley, CA 94702
(800) 666-7455

Manos Del Uruguay Yarns
DESIGN SOURCE
PO Box 770
Medford, MA 02180
(888) 566-9970

Adrienne Vittadini and
Grignasco Yarns
JCA
35 Scales Lane
Townsend, MA 01469
(800) 225-6340

Noro, Gedifra, and Klaus
Kollektion Yarns
KNITTING FEVER/EURO
YARNS
PO Box 502
Roosevelt, NY 11575-0502
(800) 645-3457
www.Knittingfever.com

Koigu Yarns
KOIGU WOOL DESIGNS
RR #1
Williamsford, Ontario N0H
2V0 Canada

Muench, Horstia, and
GGH Yarns
MUENCH
285 Bel Marin Keys, Unit J
Novato, CA 94949-576
(800) 733-9276
www.Muenchyarns.com

Prism Yarns
PRISM
2595 30th Avenue North
St. Petersburg, FL 33713
(727) 327-3100

Rowan Yarns
ROWAN USA/
WESTMINSTER FIBERS
5 Northern Boulevard Suite 3
Amherst, NH 03031
(800) 445-9276
www.KnitRowan.com

Tahki and Stacy Charles
Yarns
TAHKI/STACY CHARLES
8000 Cooper Avenue
Glendale, NY 11385
(800) 338-9276
www.TahkiStacyCharles.com

Unique Kolours Yarns
UNIQUE KOLOURS LTD
1428 Oak Lane
Downington, PA 19335
(800) 25-2DYE4
www.UniqueKolours.com

index

a

abbreviations, 19, 25, 26, 28, 49
    glossary, 44–45
Airy Wrap, 139
American method, 13, 42
armhole
    binding off, 26
    decreasing stitches, 25
    sleeve adjustment, 36
asterisks, meaning of, 45

b

backwards crochet, 32–33
Bare That Belly, 100–103
bar method (M1), 23, 24
bind off, 26–27, 44
blocking, 39
Bulky Blanket, 152–53
button bands, 38, 39
buttonholes, 28, 38

c

cardigan patterns, 79–103
cast off, 27–28, 44
cast on, 12, 16, 44
    method, 14–15
The Chunkiest of the Chunky,
    140–41
chunky yarn, 53
circular needle, 19, 44, 45
    hat pattern, 130–31
The Compromise, 121–23
A Craving to Knit, 87–91
crewneck pullovers, 66–77
    for men, 118–23
crochet hook, 29, 30, 31
crochet techniques, 31–33, 44
    shrimp stitch, 32–33
    single stitch, 31–32, 44

d

decrease (DEC), 25–26, 44
    knit 2 together, 26, 44
    slip, slip, knit, 25, 45
Design Your Own Throw, 154–55
Don't Be a Football Widow, 68–71

e

Easy, Breezy, Beautiful, 144–45
edge stitch, 44
European method, 11–12, 42

Even Daniele Did It, 56–58
The Exception to the Rule, 124–27
extra super chunky yarn, 53

f

Feeling Fuzzy, 134–35
finishing techniques, 34–39
    blocking, 39
    picking up stitches, 38–39
    sewing together, 34–37
fringe, 29–30
front/back of stitch, knitting into,
    22, 24
fundamentals, 11–45
    project tips, 48–49
    terms, 44–45
Funky Funnel-Neck Fun, 62–65
funnel-neck pullovers, 54–65

g

garter stitch, 19, 44
gauge swatch, 41–43
    importance of, 41, 48
    needle size and, 52
    pick up stitches, 39
    row gauge, 42
    stitch equation, 41, 42
    yarn weights, 53
Give the People What They Want,
    83–86
glossary, 44–45, 49

h

hats, 129–35
heavy worsted yarn, 53
He'll Wear It Every Day, 118–20
Hole-in-One, 138
holes
    picking up stitches, 39
    yarn over method, 28–29
horizontal pickup, 38–39
How Deena Got Her Ooohs and
    Aaahs, 156–57

i

increase (INC), 22–24
    bar method, 22, 23
    knitting into stitch front/back,
        22, 24
ironing. See blocking

j

Jeff's Striped Hat, 130

k

knit stitch (K), 44
    appearance, 19
    bind off, 26–27
    method, 16–17
    for ribbing, 20–21
    as right side, 44
    seed/stockinette, 45
    yarn over before, 28
knitting
    binding off, 27–28
    continuing after interruption,
        19–20
    crochet stitches, 31–33
    finishing off, 34–39
    fundamentals, 11–45
    gauge importance, 41–43
    getting started, 12–15
    glossary, 44–45
    individuality in, 42
    into front/back of stitch, 22,
        24
    markers, 50
    project tips, 48–49
    in round, 19, 44, 45
The Knitting Club's Hat, 132–33
knit 2 together (K2TOG), 26, 44

l

lace knitting, 28
left-handed knitters, 11

m

markers, knitting, 50
measurement
    of finished garment, 41
    stitch gauge, 41–43, 48
    tail, 12
    yardage, 52
men's sweaters, 117–27
mock turtleneck, 67

n

neck
    binding off, 26
    decreasing stitches, 25

finished edge, 38–39
reverse shaping, 52
See also pullover patterns
needles
    circular, 19, 44, 45
    increasing stitches on, 22, 23, 24
    knit position, 16, 17
    purl position, 18, 19
    size, 48, 52
    stitch gauge specification, 42
Not Your Standard-Issue Sweatshirt, 97–99

O

Oooh Baby, 106–8

P

patterns, 47–157
    abbreviations, 44–45, 49
    common sense use of, 49
    hat, 129–35
    poncho, 143–49
    scarf, 137–41
    specific gauge for, 42, 48
    sweater, 54–127
    terms, 50, 52
    throw, 151–57
    tips, 48–49
picking up stitches, 38–39
ponchos, 143–49
The Problem Solver, 80–82
pullover patterns, 54–127
    crewneck, 66–77
    funnel-neck, 54–65
    for men, 118–27
    V-neck, 93–103, 124–27
purl stitch (P), 44
    appearance, 19
    method, 18–19
    for ribbing, 20–21
    seed/stockinette, 45
    as wrong side, 45
    yarn over before, 28–29

R

Rectangles Only, 148–49
reverse shaping, 52
reverse stockinette stitch (REV ST ST), 44
ribbing, method, 20–21
right side (RS), 44
    sewing together on, 34
round, knitting in the, 19, 44, 45
row gauge, 42

S

scarves, 137–41
seed stitch, 44–45
sewing together, 34–37
    right side facing out, 34
    yarn type, 34
Sexy Summer Tank, 109–11
shaping, reverse, 52
shoulder seams, sewing, 35
shrimp stitch, 32–33
sides. *See* right side; wrong side
side seams, sewing, 37
single crochet stitch (SC), 31–32, 44
size. *See* measurement
sleeve
    armhole adjustment, 36
    increasing stitches, 22
    sewing, 36–37
slip knot, 12, 13
slip, slip, knit (SSK), 25, 45
stitches
    adding to, 22–24
    crochet, 31–33, 44
    decreasing, 25–26
    edge, 44
    garter, 19, 44
    gauge equation, 41, 42
    markers, 50
    picking up, 38–39
    repeating symbol, 45
    reverse stockinette, 44
    seed, 44–45
    slipping, 25
    stockinette, 19
    See also knit stitch; purl stitch
stitch gauge, 41–43, 48, 53
stockinette stitch (ST ST), 19, 45
    reverse (REV ST ST), 44
    uses, 137, 151
Stripes Are Stars, 94–96
substitute yarns, 50
Summer in the City, 112–15
super chunky yarn, 53
sweater patterns, 54–127
    cardigan, 79–103
    crewneck, 66–77
    funnel-neck, 54–65
    for men, 117–27
    tank tops, 105–15
    V-neck, 93–103, 124–27
sweaters
    fit, 41
    gauge swatch, 41–43
    neck shape/finish, 25, 26, 38–39, 52
    order of assembly, 34
    sewing together, 36–37
    yarn choice, 50

T

tail length, 12
tank tops, 105–15
A Tempting Turtleneck, 59–61
tension. *See* stitch gauge
throws, 151–57
Trick or Treat, 75–77
turtle neck, 67
    pattern, 59–61

V

vertical pick up, 38, 39
V-neck pullovers, 93–103
    for men, 124–27

W

The Weekend Warrior, 72–74
Winter Poncho, 146–47
wrong side (WS), 45

Y

yardage, 52
yarn
    adding new ball, 49
    amount, 50, 52
    arms length measure, 12
    blocking, 39
    choosing, 50
    doubled/tripled, 45
    fringe, 29–30
    markers, 50
    needle size, 52
    for sewing together, 34
    sources, 158
    substitute, 50
    weights, 53
    yardage, 52
yarn over (YO), 45
    method, 28–29